RED'S COOKBOOK
NO ROADKILL

Red's Cookbook: No Roadkill
Copyright © 2024 by Rotha J. Dawkins

Published in the United States of America

Library of Congress Control Number: 2023923111
ISBN   Paperback: 979-8-89091-660-0
ISBN   eBook: 979-8-89091-661-7

All rights reserved. No part of this publication may be reproduced, stored in a retrieval system or transmitted in any way by any means, electronic, mechanical, photocopy, recording or otherwise without the prior permission of the author except as provided by USA copyright law.

The opinions expressed by the author are not necessarily those of ReadersMagnet, LLC.

ReadersMagnet, LLC
10620 Treena Street, Suite 230 | San Diego, California, 92131 USA
1.619. 354. 2643 | www.readersmagnet.com

Book design copyright © 2024 by ReadersMagnet, LLC. All rights reserved.

Cover design by Ericka Obando
Interior design by Don De Guzman

RED'S COOKBOOK
NO ROADKILL

ROTHA J. DAWKINS

Dedicated to

My mother, Geneva Temple Dawkins (Harrelson) …

For the many years of my youth teaching me to cook and entertain. The sharing of recipes and the enjoyment of trying and testing. Then, exploring the taste of each.

Special recognition to …

To my favorite school teacher, Mrs. Theodore (Jackie) Leonard …

For being there for me in my growing years as my home economics teacher, counselor and friend. You helped put the fine touches of loving to cook in my soul. And a 'thanks' for helping open the doors of the fashion world to me.

To Mrs. Ottis (Peggy) Hedrick Hanner (deceased)

Mrs. Hedrick's impact on my life was special. She taught me to write. We spent many hours with her perfectious tutoring and corresponded over the years. She loved my cooking, I was fortunate, that at a time in my life, she married Neal Hanner and became my mother-in-law. I remember her saying to me, "Rotha, you must always write. Your technique is fine and you need to preserve knowledge and share it."

And then… As old Willie Nelson sings… "To all the guys I loved before!" … Well, let's put it like this, we were taught, the way to a man's heart is through his tummy!

ABOUT THE AUTHOR

Rotha Dawkins was born in Lexington, North Carolina. She is a graduate of Lexington High School. While still a student, and just eighteen years old, she held the first fashion show in Lexington with twenty-five gowns which she had made and designed. The show was sponsored by Belk-Martin store and was promoted statewide. Rotha received scholarships and awards for this endeavor. She then went to New York University and Mayer School of Dress Design in New York City. There she received a degree in draping and design.

Rotha has had custom design studios in New York, Great Falls, MT; Riverside, CA; Seattle, WA; Winston Salem, Greensboro, Lexington, Thomasville and Asheboro, NC.

In Seattle, she owned and operated Rotha's Commercial Design where she manufactured and designed hotel, motel and business uniforms. Also, while in Seattle, she had her own television series, "Sewing for Profit" and it was derived from her talk show, "Fashion News on TelePrompTer."

Her book, *Sewing for Profit*, was a sell out, and is in the process of being published again.

WHY NO ROAD KILL!

I've concluded… this has to be out… "road kill"! Years ago, I loved to hunt and fish, to the point I have a 'permanent sports license', which covers in season 'critters.' Menace and 'road kill' are up for the taking, I suppose.

In my finest hours of providing meat, I have done well; hunting by 'stalking, sitting, standing and trapping'; fishing streams, ponds, river, oceans and tributaries. Men have hated me on opening day of dove season; once, a fellow threw me out of the boat. Didn't matter… two things count, luck and ability!

No hunt is worth anything without the finale of cleaning and cooking. My mother is still the master of the art of cooking game; I retain the expertise in the fish department! Those of you who do hunt, know the story well.

Country living, for the sake of the unexpected, forced me to carry a 22 rifle, metal bucket, hoe and other emergency gardening and hunting tools.

It was a cool October evening, many years ago, while my children were still quite young. I had driven them to a Halloween party and was returning home.

Suddenly, a big, fat rabbit jumped in front of my car. I hit the brakes but as the tires squalled loudly, there was a big 'thump.' I could see from my rearview mirror the rabbit had had his last supper in the grass on the side. There he lay, motionless in the middle of the road.

I eased to the edge of the pavement, and even backed up a bit. Sure enough, that gorgeous, plump rabbit was now "road kill". I let the traffic pass and looked around to see that nobody was watching. After all, this was a fresh rabbit, even if the weapon was a car. I just couldn't let it go to waste.

Normally, I wouldn't bother, but rabbits in the wild were getting more and more extinct. Stray cats had taken their toll on them. Several of us hunters had band together and trapped cats then turned them over to the county pound. We had some people trapping rabbits in other areas of the county and dropping them to our area.

So, you can certainly understand that this "meal-from-the-wheel" was very special. I could almost taste that rabbit as I thought of several ways to prepare it.

I took my time getting out of my Mustang and reached into the back to get my bucket and hoe, figuring that I would flip him into the small tub. As I started toward my prey, another car showed up around the corner. This could be embarrassing if a neighbor would see you picking up "road kill." They would never believe you hit it yourself; in fact, they wouldn't want to believe that. People are nuts; they prefer to believe the worse.

It was too late to get back to the car so I started picking flowers beside the road. The old couple drove up beside me.

I could hear his window roll down and he grunted, then barked, "What 'ja doin'?"

"Nothing!" I murmured meekly, feeling like a child and continuing to keep my eye on the coveted creature. I knew old man Martin was as crazy as me and might even try to get my rabbit.

"Can't eat flowers!" he smirked. I remembered telling them once that I didn't believe in planting flowers, just things to eat.

"These are nice!" I tried to recover.

"Huh… huh… huh! We'll give you some plants! You wouldn't have to be picking on the side of the road!" he roared with laughter. "Well, pick 'em purdy!"

He left me in the smoke from his old Chevrolet. Once he was out of sight, I emptied the stupid flowers into the ditch and started to inch my way toward my special supper laying on the warm pavement ahead.

'Heck!' I thought, as I heard another car coming. Like a fool, I jumped deep into the ditch and laid down, hiding while they passed. I hoped they wouldn't run over my fat rabbit, or even worse, take him. Luck was with me. They carefully rattled out of sight.

Back out of the ditch, I stepped cautiously back to the edge of the road. Once more, I looked around to check whether anyone was in sight. I was relieved again to be alone. I adjusted my tactics and made way to the big plump hare. I would flip it into my bucket and get home with it.

The moment was finally just right. With my hoe protruding in front of me, and the bucket held out in the other hand, I felt like a knight going to war. I stealthily eased on toward Mr. Rabbit. Suddenly, I heard a big thunderous swish; then a streak of black zipped before my eyes and dropped to the road. A loud scream echoed throughout the territory as I nearly flipped into shock.

A huge, massive bird was daring me with his wings flapping and his strange crooked beak snarling, screaming and hissing. He took his stand, ordering me to move on.

I froze in fear, with my hoe pointed toward him and ready to charge. We looked at each other. His eyes were on mine and my eyes on his. Eye to eye, we raged our claim. He squawked at me and I mocked him with a similar squawk. Again, we were eye to eye in emotional combat.

Swiftly, to my most unexpected dismay, the giant bird ran to the fresh rabbit and snatched him from the ground. The big buzzard kicked off with his strong feet and legs; I watched him ascend into the spacious sky and fly off into the trees with my dinner.

The experience left me rather dumb-founded to say the least. I decided from then on there would be no "ROAD KILL" for me. To this day, I haven't even been tempted. However, I was thinking of a 'possum coat!

ABOUT THE BOOK…

My life has been spent around great cooks and wonderful food. No matter what my career is at any time, food has been important. I think we need to preserve the old time recipes of our grandmothers, mothers and friends. Thus, I have put together this recipe souce from friends and great memories. Over the years of travel and work, I have come across some special foods and learned various ways of preparing things in reasonably simple ways.

This collection of recipes is special, in the fact, that they are taste-tested and each one is excellent.

Old times forgotten will come back to you as you drift through these pages. I want you to try them all! This is what I live by. I am certain you too will be thrilled with Red's Cook Book and that you will cherish the hands of time it represents.

My travels have taken me all over the United States. Here and there, I have found great palate teasers.

Still, that big pot of pinto beans, creasy greens and cornbread taste mighty good! But then, in New York, lasagna is at its peak… Seattle can give you the finest oysters and San Francisco has that wonderful albacore…

Texas beats everybody with chili… And you can go on!

I make my own recipes from the tastes that I love! Some folks say my rolls are great. Some like my lamb. Others love my preserves and chutney. Now you have it! My secrets are out!

This book is composed especially for you. Read, enjoy and try it all! Keep in mind… If Red can do it, you can do it! Just like driving a truck… You just do it!

Best to all!

(Nostalgia)

PINTO BEANS

(Good for the Heart)

A package of dried pinto beans

Look through them for rocks, dirt clods, and bad beans. Wash real well, several times. Don't wash in pot you cook them in. Place in a large pot (four to six quart.) Cover with hot water to four inches from top.

Place on high burner and cover with lid. Bring to boil and boil for about 30-minutes.

Add:
- A large pinch of soda
- Salt to taste, (enough, not too much)
- 3 Tbsp. sugar
- 4 Tbsp. Blue Bonnet margarine

Stir well and turn heat to about 8 or medium-high.

Note: Have pot of boiling water in case you need to add. You probably will since the fast boiling evaporates much of the water. Keep adding the water and stir often. They will be done when soft to taste.

Pintos are not supposed to be hard, so cook them plenty long enough ... depending on the age of the beans as to how long they need to cook.

When they are finished cooking, check them for taste. If they taste a little flat, adjust with a bit more salt until just right. May add a bit of sugar.

WHITE LIGHTENING

(Corn Whiskey)

Harvey Easter

2 lb. ground corn 5 lb. sugar
5 gal. water ¼ pack Baker's yeast, (bulk)

Scald sugar (heat water and dissolve sugar in it.) Put into 10 gallon crock or wooden bucket or barrel. Add yeast and corn. Stir very well. Let set approximately 4 to 5 days until 'head' begins to fall. (In other words: Mixture will work, (bubble-like) bringing all the corn to the surface. When it's ready, this will fall. You can keep mesh cloth lightly covering. It's okay to look at it whenever you want to. You can see and hear it work.

CAUTION: Do NOT put tight cover on this. It will blow up!

When this is ready, pour into steel and start heating. Stir constantly until you see a slight bit of steam come off the 'mash' (mixture). Cap the steel and set your jug.

Set cap. Use water and mud to seal. Make air tight. It will dry on its own. Put tube through hole in the side. Pack mud around this.

Bring to ground or on block. (Make water trough to lay under copper pipe.)

Keep hose in trough so when the steam goes through it will become liquid and at the end of the tube you let the liquor flow into gallon jars. This will be 190 proof. You will need to cut with water about 4 to 1 or do taste test!

Makes approximately 5 gallons.

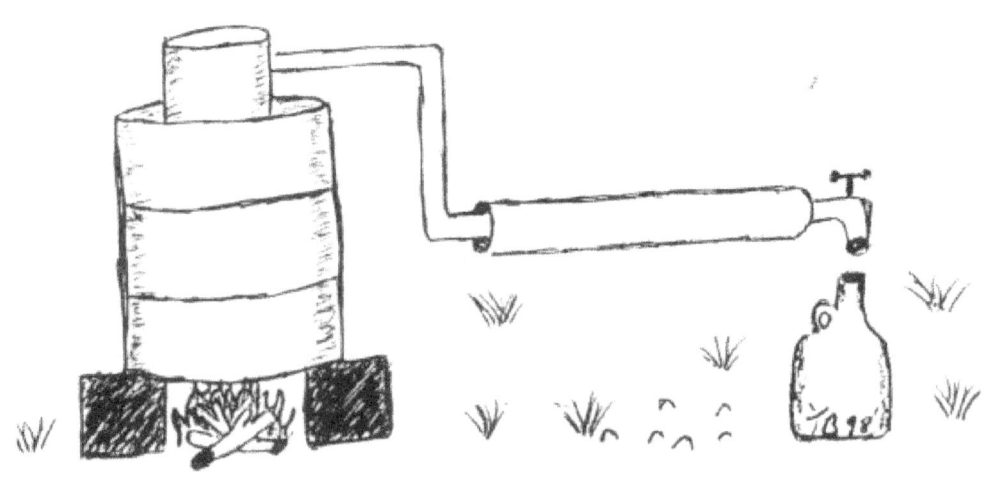

GRAPE WINE

Harvey Easter

1 peck grapes, mashed well
5 gal. water
5 lb. sugar

Mix together water and sugar. Bring to a boil until sugar dissolves. Add sugar-water to grapes which have been mashed and placed in a 10 gallon stone crock. Mix well. Cover loosely and let 'sit' 8 to 9 days (warm weather may use less time.) After it quits 'working' (bubbling), strain and enjoy! Pour into bottles or jars and cap; sealing isn't necessary.

CREASY GREENS

Rotha

Use about 3 lbs. creasy greens, adding some mustard greens to give a bigger yield for the table. Clean, trim and soak in cold water for 15 minutes. Place in a large pot with a lid, adding 1 tsp. salt or enough to taste. Boil rapidly then tum heat to medium. Cook until greens are tender. Pour off most of water. Add 3 Tbsp. butter and 1 Tbsp. bacon grease. Stir gently and return to medium heat for about 10 minutes. Stir occasionally. Do not let stick or bum! Ready when you are!

COLLARDS

Rotha

2 bunches or 6 lbs. collards, clean and trim (don't remove stalks)

Place in huge pot (canner okay, needs head room.) Boil in water covering greens. Stir occasionally to get them into the pot. Boil fast, about an hour. Keep with water; add salt to taste. They should soften (Check stem). When almost done, pour off most of water. Add ¼ c. sugar and ¼ c. margarine. Finish cooking on medium heat. Cut up to serve.

OLD FASHIONED LYE SOAP

(Not Edible)

1 can lye 1 pk. hot water, spring or rain
2 or 3 lb. lard, or old grease

Melt lard in cast iron wash pot. Dissolve lye in hot water; let cool. Pour lye solution in a slow, easy stream into melted fat, stirring constantly. Continue stirring until cool. Pour into boxes that have been dipped in cold water. Cut in desired size squares when cold and set.

NOTE: Make in shrinking of the moon. Do not use aluminum foil. Do not stir with red oak stick; use only a white oak stick.

GRANDFATHER TEMPLE'S FRIED APPLES

Rinsey John Allen Temple

1 Tbsp. Crisco oil
½ stick butter, (country butter)
5 or 6 apples (Delicious), cored, peeled & thinly sliced
¼ c. sugar
juice of ½ lemon

In a skillet heat Crisco; add butter and melt. When Medium hot, throw in apples. Cook and gently stir occasionally. Let them get slightly brown, (butter can burn easily). When they are tender when tested with a fork and slightly transparent looking, sprinkle lemon over and sift sugar over all. Turn gently several times. Serve hot with meal.

SLAW

1 head cabbage, shredded	¼ c. sugar
1 med. onion	1 c. vinegar
1 med. green pepper, chopped	½ c. Wesson oil
1 tsp. salt	2 tsp. celery seed

Heat to boiling the vinegar, oil, celery seed, sugar and salt. Cool and pour over cabbage, onion and pepper. Will keep 3 to 4 weeks in the refrigerator sealed in a fruit jar.

QUICK FRUIT CAKE

Rotha

1 lb. butter	nuts
12 eggs	1 box white raisins
4 c. flour	1 box dark raisins
4 c. sugar	dates
1 c. syrup	figs
1 tsp. soda	red & green glazed
3 tsp. nutmeg	pineapple
2 tsp. cinnamon	candied cherries

Dissolve soda in syrup. Cream butter and sugar. Add eggs, syrup (with soda) and part of flour. Mix nuts and fruits in flour heavily. Add remaining flour. Bake 1 ½ hours at 350°F.

A TRUCK DRIVER'S DREAM; BUTTER-PECAN CAKE

2 sticks butter	2 ½ c. sifted plain flour
2 c. brown sugar	½ c. plain yogurt
5 eggs, (separate 3 whites and set aside)	½ c. sour cream
	¼ c. buttermilk
1 block semi-sweet chocolate	1 tsp. soda
¼ c. black coffee	1 tsp. vinegar

Cream together butter and brown sugar. Add 2 whole eggs and 3 yolks to creamed mixture. Melt semi-sweet chocolate in black coffee. Add to creamed mixture. Combine yogurt, sour cream and buttermilk. Add alternately with flour to first creamed mixture. Dissolve soda in vinegar. Add to creamed mixture. Add 3 whipped egg whites last. Bake in 5 or 6 layers at 350°F for 15 to 20 minutes each.

LAYER ICING:

2 Tbsp. cornstarch	1 ¼ c. sugar
1 c. water	1 tsp. brandy flavoring
1 c. margarine	1 c. chopped pecans

Mix cornstarch and water. Cook until thick. Cream together margarine and sugar but do not melt the margarine. Add cornstarch mixture and brandy flavoring to creamed mixture. Beat till thick and well blended. Add pecans; spread on layers.

ICING FOR SIDES & TOP:

1 ½ stick butter
1 ½ c. powdered sugar
½ c. powdered cocoa
1 egg

1 tsp. vanilla
1 ½ tsp hot black coffee
chopped pecans

Cream together butter (not melted) and powdered sugar. Add cocoa. Beat in egg and vanilla. Smooth in black coffee. Ice top and sides of cake. Sprinkle with chopped pecans.

CHICKEN DRESSING

2 chickens, (fryers), boiled
1 loaf bread, (3 days old, leave in open pan to dry)
½ lb. box crackers
8 eggs
2 Tbsp. basil leaves
3 Tbsp. chopped parsley
2 tsp. baking powder
1 tsp. yellow food color
3 qt. chicken broth

Boil chickens until done. Remove meat from bones; set aside. Cube bread into small pieces; crush crackers; mix together, handling lightly. Add basil, parsley and baking powder. Then add eggs, one at a time; mix gently. Add food coloring to broth; stir into dry mixture. Mix as little as possible. HANDLE ONLY ENOUGH TO BLEND. Grease with Crisco a large baking pan. Place chicken liberally in bottom. Pour dressing on top. Bake for approximately 45 minutes in an oven of 450°F.

SUGAR CURED HAM

1 joint (250 lb.) hog
1 pt. salt
1 Tbsp. red pepper

2 Tbsp. black pepper
3 Tbsp. brown sugar

Mix all dry ingredients. Round the tablespoons up. Don't level them off Rub dry mixture on the skin side first, until the skin is moist: repeat on opposite side. Be sure to fill the joint end full. Wrap tight with brown paper; tie tightly. Put in a white sack with the joint end down. Let lay with skin down for 54 hours. Hand up with joint down until about June (approximately six months to cure or longer).

NOTE: Curing meat should be started in the fall, October or November, when it starts to become cool.

PORK CRACKLIN'S AND LARD

Use 5 lb. meat skins. Place in large iron skillet. Cook at boiling temperature; hot! Fry until crisp. Separate grease, which should be poured off into containers. (This is lard.)

NOTE: For use in cornbread, crumble the cracklin's.)

CRACKLIN' PUDDIN'

2 lb. pork backbones or neckbones
1 lb. pork liver
1 c. pork crackin's
1 tsp. ground sage
1 sm. onion, chopped
1 sm. pod dry red pepper, chopped fine
salt to taste
cornmeal

Boil pork and liver together until tender. Remove meat from borth. Save broth. Take 1 cup of meat from bone and add to liver which has been crumbled. Combine meat mixture with sage, crackings, onion, pepper and salt to 1 quart of broth. Bring to a boil. Stir in cornmeal until thick. Pour into dish and let cool. Slice and fry.

SWEET PICKLE PEACHES

1 c. vinegar
6 c. water
5 c. sugar

3 tsp. pickling spice
6 qt. peaches, peeled

Pack jars with peaches. Combine vinegar, water, sugar and pickling spice. Heat until sugar is melted. Pour over peaches and seal. Process in water bath for about 5 minutes.

DILL PICKLES

whole cucumbers dill
1 tsp. salt vinegar
1 tsp. sugar

Wash cucumbers and place in a pan. Cover with boiling water. Let stand until cool enough to handle with hands. Put in hot jars and add salt, sugar and dill (to suit your taste) to 1 pint. Cover with boiling vinegar (½ vinegar and ½ water.) Seal.

BREAD AND BUTTER PICKLES

DAY ONE:

9 lb. cucumbers
1 ½ c. pickling lime
2 ½ gal. cold water

Soak cucumbers in mixture of pickling lime and water for 24 hours. Rinse thoroughly several times. (This process makes cucumbers a good texture. Be careful handling so as not to break. They will be brittle.)

DAY TWO:

10 med. onions, sliced
2 lg. bell peppers, chopped
5 med. green tomatoes, sliced
2 qt. white distilled vinegar
3 ½ lb. sugar
1 Tbsp. salt
3 Tbsp. mustard seed
*3 Tbsp. celery seed
1 Tbsp. turmeric

Add rinsed cucumbers to onions, bell peppers and green tomatoes. Cover all with ice water. Let stand for 3 hours. Drain well. Add vinegar, sugar, salt, mustard seed, celery seed and turmeric. Stir to mix and let stand overnight.

*If you like celery use this amount, otherwise add 1 more tablespoon of pickling spice on third day.

DAY THREE:

Add 4 Tbsp. pickling spice. Let stand overnight.

DAY FOUR:

Bring all to a boil; let boil for 20 minutes. Pack in jars and seal. (Approximately 12 pints.)

SASSAFRAS JELLY

2 c. strong sassafras tea
1 pkg. powdered pectin
3 c. strained honey
2 Tbsp. sassafras root bark, grated

Put sassafras tea in cooking pan. Add pectin; bring to a slight boil. Add honey and root bark powder; simmer 6 minutes. Put in hot jelly glasses and seal.

BLUE RIBBON FIG PRESERVES

10 lb. figs, halved   ½ c. water
5 ½ lb. sugar

Combine figs, sugar and water. Let stand overnight (or 18 hours). Next day bring to a boil; reduce heat and cook for 2 ½ hours, stirring occasionally being careful not to let stick. Pack in jars and seal.

ROTHA'S ORANGE MARMALADE

Rotha

12 to 14 oranges (equal to 4 to 4 ½ c.)
½ c. water

juice of 2 lemons
7 c. sugar
1 pkg. pectin

Peel half the oranges, removing seeds, ends and bad spots from all. Cut into wedges.

In blender combine orange wedges, water and lemon juice. Measure to 4 ½ to 5 ½ cups total.

Pour into heavy, deep cast aluminum pot. Add sugar. Bring to rolling boil over medium heat. Cook 3 minutes. Let sit off heat for 20 minutes. Add pectin; boil and stir 3 minutes. Turn heat off; skim off and stir for 7 minutes. Pour in jars and seal.

PEAR HONEY

Rotha

3 lb. ripe pears   juice of 1 lemon
1 c. pineapple   5 c. sugar

Wash, peel, core and slice pears. (Slice before measuring.) Chop pears and pineapple. Add lemon juice and sugar. Cook for 20 minutes. Put in jars and process in water bath canner for 5 minutes.

GREEN PEPPER JELLY

6 lg. green peppers, cut in pieces
1 ½ c. cider vinegar, (4% to 5% acid strength)
6 c. sugar
½ tsp. salt
1 tsp. crushed red pepper
green food coloring

Put half the green peppers and half the vinegar into blender. Cover and process until pepper is liquefied. Pour into a sauce pan. Repeat with remaining pepper and vinegar. Add the red pepper, sugar and salt. Bring to a boil and add pectin. Boil until it thickens when dropped from spoon about 20 minutes.

Add a few drops of green food coloring. Pour into sterilized jars leaving ¼-inch head space and seal. Makes 4 half-pints.

ROTHA'S BEST STRAWBERRY PRESERVES

Rotha

2 qt. strawberries, sliced   juice of 1 ½ lemons
7 c. sugar   1 Tbsp. margarine

Pour strawberries into a heavy pot. Add sugar to berries, stirring well. Let stand for 30 minutes. Separate berries from juice, by straining. Blend berries for about 5 seconds, keeping coarse. Pour berries and juice back into pot and stir well while bring to a boil. Add lemon juice. Cook over medium heat for 1 ½ to 2 hours from boiling point. Add margarine; stir. Pour into jars and seal

*For an unusual flavor add:

½ pkg. frozen coconut and 1 tsp. almond flavoring to ¼ of pureed mixture. Stir well; cook for 15 to 20 minutes. Put into jars and seal.

PEPPER RELISH

Rotha

12 sweet red peppers	2 Tbsp. salt
12 sweet green peppers	1 qt. vinegar
14 med. size onions	3 c. sugar

Grind peppers and onions. Pour boiling water over them; let stand 5 minutes and drain. Again cover with boiling water for 10 minutes; drain again. Add vinegar, sugar and salt. Bring to a boil and cook for 20 minutes. Pour into sterilized jars and seal.

GREEN TOMATO RELISH

Rotha

8 c. chopped green tomatoes
1 ½ c. chopped onion
½ c. chopped sweet red pepper
½ c. chopped green pepper
½ c. sugar

1 c. light com syrup
1 Tbsp. salt
1 Tbsp. white mustard seed
½. tsp. white pepper

In a large sauce pot, stir together the tomato, onion, red and green pepper, sugar, corn syrup, vinegar, salt, mustard seed and white pepper. Bring to a boil; reduce heat and boil gently until vegetables are tender-crisp, about 45 minutes. Leaving ¼ inch head space, ladle into clean, hot ½ pint wide mouth jars. Seal according to manufacturer's directions. Process in boiling water for 10 minutes. Cool on wire racks or folded cloth. Label and store in the refrigerator. In this case, processing is not necessary. Makes 3 (½ pint) jars.

SQUASH RELISH

Rotha

8 c. shredded squash
2 c. onion
2 green peppers
1 red pepper
1 hot pepper, chopped

2 ½ c. sugar
2. c vinegar
2 tsp. mustard seed
½. tsp. dry mustard

Layer squash, onion and pepper. Sprinkle with salt. Let stand for 1 hour. Drain off salt. Cover in ice water for about 15 minutes. Mix sugar, vinegar, mustard seed and dry mustard. Bring to a boil. Put squash, onion and pepper in pot and bring to a boil. Pack in pint jars; seal and put in hot water bath for 10 minutes.

CHOW CHOW

Rotha

1 gal. green tomatoes
6 lg. onions
6 or 8 lg. sweet peppers
3 or 4 lb. head cabbage

Chop and mix well green tomatoes, onions, sweet peppers and cabbage. Divide into two large kettles. To each add:

2 ½ c. vinegar
3 c. sugar (or more to taste)
½ box pickling spice
½. tsp. mustard seed
½ tsp. celery seed
1 Tbsp. salt
1 tsp. turmeric, if desired

Boil 15 minutes. Seal in sterilized jars. Makes 24 quarts.

SUPER CHOW CHOW

Rotha

1 Tbsp. salt
1 peck green tomatoes
3 lb. (10 med.) onions
2 heads cabbage
12 sweet green peppers

12 sweet red peppers
8 hot peppers
3 Tbsp. mustard seed
4 Tbsp. pickling spice
10 c. sugar
16 c. vinegar

Put tomatoes, onions, cabbage and peppers through food processor. Drain juice and divide in half. Pour into 2 stainless steel pots on stove top. Add 5 c. sugar and 8 c. vinegar to each pot. Add mustard seed and pickling spices (which have been divided and tied in a small cloth bag) to each pot. Cook about 30 minutes. Put in jars and seal.

DR. TREDWAY'S FAVORITE CHUTNEY

Rotha

4 cucumbers, chopped
8 peaches, peeled and chopped
1 ¼ qt. tomatoes, ripe, peeled and chopped
1 ½ qt. apples, peeled, cored and chopped
juice of 1 lemon
3 sweet peppers, red or green
1 hot pepper, chopped very fine, optional
1 (16 oz.) pkg. raisins
1 c. chopped onion

3 c. vinegar
3 c. brown sugar
1 Tbsp. pickling spice
1 Tbsp. allspice
¾ Tbsp. garlic powder
¾ Tbsp. nutmeg
½ tsp. cloves, optional
½ tsp. black pepper
juice of 1 ½ lemon
½ rind of lemon, grated

Combine, cucumbers, peaches, tomatoes, apples, juice of 1 lemon, sweet peppers, hot pepper, raisins and onion. This should not be done in a blender but with a food chopper or by hand so you will get a blend of flavors. Keep pieces thin, and even-sized if possible. In a large pot combine vinegar, brown sugar, pickling spice, allspice, garlic powder, nutmeg, cloves, black pepper, juice of 1 ½ lemons and grated lemon rind. Place on medium heat; bring to a boil. Cook for 5 minutes. Steep for 11 minutes. Pour over first mixture using a large cooking pot (stainless steel or enamel). Bring all ingredients to a rapid simmer. Cook in this way for about 15 minutes or until raisins are done. Seal in pint or smaller jars. (Treat as you would pickle.) Chutney is wonderful with most meats but especially lamb. I was introduced to chutney through a lady in Seattle who would not part with her recipe but this is every bit as good as I remember Mrs. Pindleton's chutney.

ROTHA'S PEACH CHUTNEY

(as a meat sauce)

Rotha

2 qt. peaches, peeled, chopped	1 c. sugar
1 qt. tomatoes, peeled, chopped	½ c. molasses
juice of 1 lemon	2 Tbsp. pickling spice
2 sweet peppers, chopped fine	1 Tbsp. garlic powder
1 hot pepper, chopped fine	2 Tbsp. nutmeg
1 (24 oz.) box raisins	1 Tbsp. allspice
1 c. onion, chopped fine	2 tsp. cloves
3 c. vinegar	1 Tbsp. black Pepper
2 c. brown sugar	1 Tbsp. dry mustard
	juice of 1 lemon

Combine peaches, tomatoes, juice of 1 lemon, sweet peppers, hot pepper, raisins and onion; set aside. In a large stainless steel or enamel pot combine vinegar, sugars, molasses, pickling spice, garlic powder, nutmeg, allspice, cloves, black pepper, dry mustard and juice of 1 lemon. Bring to a boil, cooking for 10 minutes.

Rest 10 minutes; pour over first mixture and return to a fast boil, stirring occasionally for 25 minutes.

Place in jars and cap. Treat likes pickles.

SWAMP SOUP

Rotha

You may use the crock pot or place this in a big pot on top of the stove.

6 single frog legs, cleaned and skinned	2 large baking potatoes, clean and cut into wedges
3 fifteen-inch trout (or close), cleaned, leaving on head and tail	3 sticks celery, cut up
2 c. turtle meat	1 lg. tomato, not over-ripe
6 clams (in shell)	seasoning of salt, pepper, garlic powder, parsley flakes, to taste
4 oysters (in shell)	½ lemon juice
½ c. dried baby lima beans	1 lg. onion, cut into wedges
	6 c. water

Start these items, adding water if needed:

Turtle meat, lima beans, potato, celery and seasonings. Cook in three cups of water for 2 hours on high heat (in crock pot). On stove top boil on medium heat for 1 hour.

Add balance of ingredients for simmer cooking about 3- 4 hours in the crock or simmer on top of stove about 3 hours or until done. Place carefully into big serving dish/bowl and ladle at table.

HAWAIIAN LOVE POTION

8 slices pineapple and juice
1 c. (50) dates, chopped
¼ c. brown sugar
¼ stick margarine

¼ c. walnuts, chopped
⅛ c. wafer crumbs
1 Kiwi, peeled & sliced

In saute pan, place 1 cup juice, pineapple, dates, brown sugar and margarine. Bring to a boil; turn heat down slightly and stir constantly, turning pineapple over several times. Gook about 3 minutes. Place wafer crumbs, Kiwi and walnuts in 4 dessert dishes and pour potion equally divided into each. Serves four.

ICE SHAKE

2 slices pineapple.
½ can peaches
2 Tbsp. sugar
2 Tbsp. milk
½ tsp. vanilla flavoring
6 cubes ice

Combine fruits, sugar, milk, flavoring and ice in Osterizer. Mix for approximately 2 minutes or until ice is mushy. For another flavor, used desired fruit. May freeze in bulk for ice cream.

PEACH FUZZ

1 sm. 6 oz. can Lemonade concentrate
1 sm. 6 oz. can Gin or Vodka

1 ½. pt. frozen peaches
Ice

Blend together lemonade concentrate and gin. Add frozen peaches and blend slightly. Add enough ice to fill blender and blend well until ice is finely crushed.

RUSSIAN TEA

1 gal. water
4 lg. tea bags
3 ½ c. sugar
1 qt. apple juice
1 lg. can pineapple juice
1 (12. oz,) can orange juice concentrate

1 c. lemon juice, fresh or Minute Maid
2 c. water
4 tsp. whole cloves
4 tsp. broken cinnamon sticks

Bring 1 gallon of water to a boil. Steep tea bags for five minutes in water. Add sugar and apple juice; return to boiling point. Add pineapple, orange and lemon juice. In another pan mix 2 cups water, cloves and broken cinnamon sticks. Simmer for 20 minutes. Strain into first juice and tea mixture. Makes 2 gallons.

SASSAFRAS TEA

2 - 3 sassafras roots, 2 to 3 inches' long   1 qt. water   sugar to sweeten

Boil roots in water until the tea is dark in color. Remove from heat; strain into gallon pitcher. Add enough water to finish filling pitcher. Sweeten as you would regular tea. Serve hot or cold.

NOTE: These roots may be boiled over and over for several days as the flavor increases with successive boilings. Sassafras roots should be gathered in the early spring before the sap rises.

STRAWBERRY PUNCH

2 lg. cans pineapple juice
2 lg. can frozen orange juice
juice of 6 lemons
juice of 6 limes
1 qt. water

2 c. sugar
1 lg, can sliced pineapple
2 pkg. frozen strawberries
½ lb. grapes, green

Blend juices; add sugar and water. Add strawberries, grapes and pineapple.

Red food coloring can be added if desired.

PARTY FRUIT PUNCH

2 lg. cans (12 oz.) frozen orange juice concentrate
3 sm. cans (6 oz.) lemonade concentrate
2 lg. cans pineapple juice
1 c. sugar (or less) Ginger Ale

Mix the orange juice and lemonade with the water (as called for on the can). Add the pineapple juice and sugar. Stir well, till sugar is dissolved. When ready to serve, add a bottle of ginger ale to each gallon of punch. (You can stretch this by using more ginger ale or even adding a little water.)

Make a frozen punch ring to keep this cold. Put water in a tube cake pan and color this with some food coloring. You can add any fruit that you like: cherries, slices of lemon or orange or pieces of fresh mint leaves in the summer are pretty, etc. Note: You will only need a few drops of cake coloring to color the water… This punch is yellow in color but you may change the color. Recipe makes approximately 2 gallons.

PINEAPPLE PUNCH

2 sm. pkg. lemon flavored Jello
3 ½ c. sugar
10 c. hot water
4 sm. cans frozen lemonade
3 c. canned orange juice
2 #2 cans pineapple juice
1 qt. ginger ale, chilled

Dissolve gelatin and sugar in hot water; cool. Add juices; chill. Add ginger ale just before serving.

APPLE SALAD

3 Red Delicious apples, unpeeled and cube
1 can pineapple chunks, drain, (saving juice)
1 c. cheddar cheese, shredded
1 c. pecans, chopped

5 c. sugar
2 Tbsp. plain flour
1 egg, beaten
1 c. juice, (add water if not enough for 1 cup)

Layer apples, pineapple, cheddar cheese and pecans in baking dish. For custard combine, sugar, flour, egg and juice. Cook over low-medium heat until thick. Cool slightly. Pour over layered dish.

GUACAMOLE SALAD

1 (4 oz.) can taco sauce
2 c. mashed avocados
1 tsp. onion juice

few drops lemon juice
¼ tsp. garlic salt

Combine all ingredients and serve on lettuce with corn chips or tostadas.

HOT VEGETABLE SALAD

In a large oven dish place a layer of:

½ (3 Tbsp.) butter and oil

Layer with:

1 head of cabbage, thickly sliced, with core removed	1 lb. shredded & salted potatoes, pre-cooked halfway
½ pkg. sliced mushrooms	4 carrots, thinly sliced
1 med. onion, sliced thick	

Mix well together:

1 ½ Tbsp. cornstarch   1 c. water

Pour over top of layered ingredients. Sprinkle with salt and pepper. Cover tight and bake in 375°F oven for 20 – 30 minutes. Serve from cooking dish.

CHICKEN SALAD

3 c. diced, cooked chicken
4 boiled eggs, chopped
½ c. celery, chopped
½. c. olives, chopped
½ c. pecans, chopped

½ c. sweet pickles, chopped
1 c. pineapple tidbits
1 c. apple, chopped
½ c. Helman's mayonnaise to mix

Combine all ingredients well. Chill and serve.

HOT CHICKEN SALAD

4 chicken breasts or 1 whole chicken, cooked & diced
1 can cream of chicken soup
1 c. celery, diced
½ c. slivered almonds, toasted & broken
½ tsp. salt
¼ tsp. pepper
1 Tbsp. lemon juice
¾ c. mayonnaise
2. hard boiled eggs, chopped
1 sm. can sliced mushrooms
1 c. brown rice, cooked
1 c. crushed potato chips, (optional for topping)

Mix all ingredients well. Turn into greased casserole dish. Bake at 375°F for 45 minutes, leaving covered for the first 30 minutes. This may be served with a can of Cream of Chicken soup as a sauce. NOTE: This is a good recipe for "by-gosh-and- by-golly" substitutions: English walnuts instead of almonds, white rice instead of brown, pimentoes, with or without the mushrooms.

QUICK GUACAMOLE

1 ripe avocado
½ c. sm. curd cottage cheese
⅓ c. hot picante sauce or Salsa
½ tsp. minced seeded jalapeno pepper, opt.
Tortilla chips or raw vegetables

In a bowl, mash the avocado. Stir in cottage cheese and picante sauce. Add jalapeno, if desired. Serve with chips or vegetables. Yield: about 1 ½ cups.

JELLO!

1 can pineapple, drained
1 pkg. lime Jello

Prepare Jello according to package directions. Add pineapple and chill until firm. Slice and serve.

OTHER IDEAS:

STRAWBERRY JELLO SALAD:

Use 1 c. frozen strawberries in place of 1 c. water when preparing Strawberry Flavored Jello.

VEGETABLE JELLO SALAD

Cook broccoli until tender. Cool and drain. Prepare lemon Jello according to package directions. Pour into mold. When slightly firm add broccoli and chill until firm.

Try some of your own ideas!

DIOR SALAD

1 avocado, remove peeling & seed sliced thin
½ c. coconut, shredded

1 c. pineapple tidbits, drain & dry with paper towel
½ sm. lettuce head, shredded
6 cherries, halved

Mix all ingredients. When ready to serve, combine the following:

½ c. mayonnaise
2 Tbsp. water

2 Tbsp. catsup
squirt of lemon

Toss with salad and serve.

PEA SALAD A LA GOOD FRIEND

1 lettuce head, shredded fine
2 sm. or 1 lg. can green peas, drained
1 onion, sliced
½ c. celery, chopped fine
¼ c. green pepper, chopped
¼ c. carrots, chopped fine
½ tsp. garlic powder, sprinkled in
1 c. mayonnaise
Parmesan cheese

Layer each of the above ingredients into a 2 quart bowl in order listed. Sprinkle cheese generously. May be made ahead of time. Place in refrigerator covered with plastic wrap or in an airtight container. An excellent party salad.

BACON SALAD

1 head lettuce, shredded
1 tomato, diced

5 Spring onions, sliced, using some tops
6 slices bacon, cut into diced bits

Place lettuce, tomato, and onions in a salad bowl and keep refrigerated. Fry bacon on medium heat until crisp. Do not burn!

Combine together:

¼ c. wine vinegar
¼ tsp. salt
2 Tbsp. sugar

2 Tbsp. cold water
½ tsp. black pepper

Pour over salad: toss, adding hot bacon bits & drippings.

DILL DIP FOR VEGETABLES

1 pt. mayonnaise
1 pt. sour cream
1 Tbsp. dried parsley
3 Tbsp. grated. onion
3 Tbsp. dill weed
1 ½ Tbsp. seasoned salt

Combine all ingredients and refrigerate. Makes 4 cups.

CHILI CON QUESO DIP

1 lg. onion, chopped
1 clove garlic, chopped
2 Tbsp. butter or margarine
1 ½ c. canned tomatoes, drained

1 (4 oz.) can chopped green chili peppers
1 lb. Velveeta cheese

In heavy skillet or in top of double boiler, cook onion and garlic in butter. Add tomatoes which have. been mashed with fork. Add peppers and cheese; cook over low heat until cheese melts, Serve warm. Great with crackers and chips. Keeps for weeks in the refrigerator.

BEEF DIP

2 pkgs. Buddig beef, (or use the dried, packaged beef), chopped fine
1 ½ c. sour cream
1 c. Duke's mayonnaise
3 Tbsp. Spring onion, chopped, using some of the green top
3 Tbsp. Spring onion, chopped, using some of the green top)
1 pkg. Lipton Vegetable Soup Mix, (the dry kind)
1 tsp. dill weed

Combine all ingredients. Chill over night before serving.

SPINACH BEEF DIP

1 (10 oz.) pkg. frozen spinach, thawed & chopped
1 (8 oz.) pkg. cream cheese, softened
1 c. mayonnaise
½ c. green onions, chopped
1 Tbsp. dill weed
1 (2 ½ oz.) jar sliced, dried beef, rinsed & chopped
Assorted crackers

Combine spinach, cream cheese, mayonnaise, green onions and dill weed in container of electric blender; process on high speed 1 to 2 minutes or until smooth and creamy. Fold in dried beef Chill. Serve with crackers. Yield: 3 cups.

RED'S BARBEQUE DIP

Rotha

1 c. vinegar
1 pt. water
salt to taste
1 stick margarine
juice of 1 lemon

dash hot pepper
¼ c. sugar
1 c. (more or less)
Hunt's catsup

Stir together all ingredients. Bring to a boil then put on low heat. Simmer for 30 minutes.

This sauce is great to baste meats as they are being grilled or charcoaled. You can also pour over chicken or roast, wrap in foil. Bake at 375°F oven for 1 hour (roast—20 minutes per lb.)

CATFISH STEW

12 (about 2 lbs.) catfish, cleaned

6 c. water
1 tsp. salt or salt substitute

Boil 20 minutes at high temperature. Remove bone and skin. Return meat to pot.

Add:

½ c. cooked or frozen peas
1 med. onion, chopped
6 more c. water
½ tsp. pepper
1 very sm. can mushroom

12 peppercorns
2 Tbsp. corn margarine
½ tsp. garlic powder
2 thinly sliced potatoes, if you wish

Boil 20 minutes, stirring often. Add salt to taste.

HALIBUT STEW FOR SIX

Rotha

¼ lb. Halibut
6 c. water
¾ tsp. salt

Boil for ½ hour at medium high temperature. Remove bone and skin from fish. Cut up and return to pot.

Add:

2 lg. potatoes, cut up   ½ tsp. pepper
½ c. baby carrots   ¼ c. sliced, fresh mushrooms
1 med. Onion, cut up   12 peppercorns
6 c. water   2 Tbsp. butter
½ tsp. garlic powder

Boil for 20 minutes, Stir often. Add more salt to taste. Soup will slightly thicken when done.

POTATO/CORN SOUP

3 lg. potatoes cut into thick slices
1 pkg. frozen corn
1 lg. onion, sliced
1 tsp. salt (to taste)
1 tsp. pepper
1 qt. water
¼ c. fresh parsley
1 beef bouillon cube

Cook together on medium heat for 45 minutes or until potatoes are done.

Add:

½ c. water   2 tsp. corn starch

Blend into soup stock. Serves 4 people.

OYSTER STEW

Rotha

½ pt. oysters
½ stick butter or margarine
½ tsp. black pepper

Place together in pot and simmer with lid on for about 8 minutes (until oyster's wrinkle on edges)

Add:

1 can evaporated milk (fat free)
¼ c. catsup
1 ½ c. homogenized milk
1 can water

Heat to the point of boiling. Serve with crackers.

SASSY LADY'S VEGGIE-CHICKEN STEW

Rotha

4 - 6 chicken breast-rib bones, after removing serving meat
2 lg. potatoes, thick sliced
¼ c. fresh parsley, chopped
2 sm. carrots, thick sliced
½ c. frozen green beans
1 lg. onion, sliced
½ tsp. salt (to taste)
10 peppercorns
¼ tsp. garlic powder

Boil chicken bones for 45 minutes to 1 hour. Remove bones and fat from soup. Take whatever lean meat you can find and put back with soup stock. Let soup stand, then put in freezer to set up liquid fat. Skim off—add all above ingredients and cook on medium heat for 45 minutes to 1 hour.

OIL BOTTLE STEW

When you purchase whole chickens, cut up or not, there are always parts that are not used for frying and different dishes. Make it a habit to save these in a separate bag in the freezer. Especially, the far south end of the bird flyin north, the oil bottle. Collect about six of these along with a couble backs and necks. You can add any other pierces of fat or wing tips. Keep frozen until needed

6 (at least) oil bottles of chicken	salt to taste, (when adding the water)
2 backs of chicken	water to well cover, (add 1 pt. when half boiled)
2 necks of chicken, (plus any other parts you choose to add)	5 peppercorns
1 c. uncooked rice, brown or white, (wash before use)	2 tsp. parsley
	1 sm. onion well diced

Defrost chicken in microwave oven about 3 minutes if frozen. In large pan fill with cold water and add 1 Tbsp. Clorox. Wash chicken pieces completely; pour off water and rinse well.

Place in pot and cover with three inches of water. Add salt and peppercorns. Bring to rolling boil (uncovered). Let boil for fifteen minutes, or until bird is done.

Take bird from pot and remove lean meat from bones and return meat to broth. Dispose of bones and fat. Add rest of ingredients listed above. Cook, on medium heat for about twenty minutes, doneness with rice. Serve hot with bread or toast.

RAINY DAY CHICK-VEG SOUP

Rotha

1 Ib. chicken backs or wings
2 qt. water
salt to taste
12 pepper corns
½ Tbsp. parsley flakes
3 lg. potatoes, diced

1 sm. carrot, sliced
5 oz. lima beans, frozen
5 oz. peas, frozen
2 stalks celery, diced, optional
½ onion, chopped
½ tsp. garlic powder

Cook chicken, peppercorns and parsley flakes in water with parsley on medium heat for about an hour or until chicken is done. Remove chicken from pot and de-bone.

Return the meat back into the pot with the original soup. Add potatoes, carrots, lima beans, peas, celery, onion and garlic powder. Add enough water to well cover vegetables. Bring to a boil and cook at medium heat for' about a half hour. Serves four.

EARLY BIRD'S WONDER BREAD

Rotha

Sift together:

2 ½ c. self-rising flour	1 Tbsp. (level) baking powder
½ tsp. salt.	¼ tsp. soda

Add:

½ c. Crisco	2 lg. eggs or 3 small
1 c. sour cream	½ to 1 c. homogenized milk

Mix well, adding milk ½ cup at a time. Mixture should be too thin to roll out. Spoon out into well greased "12 muffin tin." Bake at 410 to 425 degrees for approximately 20 to 30 minutes. They should almost triple the original size.

BANANA NUT BREAD

¾ c. sugar
¼ c. butter
1 egg
2 c. flour

½ tsp. soda
¼ tsp. salt
⅔ c. broken nut meats
3 ripe bananas

Cream butter and sugar, add egg. Mash bananas and add to sugar mixture. Sift dry ingredients, add alternately with milk to creamed mixture. Add nuts, Bake in greased loaf pan in 350 degrees' oven for 45 minutes.

BREAKFAST RUM BUNS

1 c. scalded milk	1 egg
½ c. granulated sugar	1 ½ tsp. rum extract
¼ c. shortening crisco	3 ½ c. sifted flour
1 ¼ tsp. salt	4 tbsp. butter, melted
1 cake of compressed yeast	½ c. raisins, cut up

Pour scalded milk over ¼ cup of sugar, shortening add salt. Cool to lukewarm and crumble yeast into it. Beat with a rotary beater until smooth. Add beaten egg and rum extract. Add ½ the flour and beat with rotary beater until smooth. Add remaining flour and mix until smooth.

Cover with a towel and let rise in a warm place (80 to 85°F) until double in bulk – about 3 hours.

Roll dough into two strips, each 12" long, ½" thick and 4" wide. Brush top with melted butter and sprinkle with ¼ cup sugar and raisins. Roll up, pulling dough out at edges to keep it uniform. Should be 15" long when rolled.

Cut rolls in crosswise slices, ¾" thick. Place in 3" greased muffin tins; cover with a towel and let rise in a warm place until double in bulk. Bake in moderately hot oven of 400°F for 15 to 20 minutes.

As soon as rolls are removed from oven brush top with icing made of 1 cup confectioners sugar, 2 Tbsp. hot water and 1 tsp. rum extract.

RED'S CORNBREAD MUFFINS

From Grandfather Temple
via Rotha J. Dawkins

2 ½ c. cornmeal, self-rising   1 tsp. salt
½ c. flour, self-rising   ⅓ c, sugar

Combine into sifter. Sift into bowl. Add:

1 egg, slightly beaten   1 ¼ c. buttermilk
½ c. Crisco shortening   ½ c. milk

Squish together with one hand. Mix well to get all lumps out. Flop with hand. Add more buttermilk to get right texture if needed. Should not be stiff. Grease muffin tins and fill to a little less than ¼" from top. Bake in 450-degree oven. (For about 20 to 30 mins.)

ALABAMA HUSHPUPPIES

1 ¾ c. cornmeal
1 tsp. salt
4 Tbsp. flour
1 tsp. baking powder

6 tbsp. chopped onion
1 egg, beaten
1 ¾ c. boiling water

Mix and sift all dry ingredients. Add chopped onion and beaten egg. Pour boiling water over this and stir constantly until mixture is smooth. Drop by spoonfuls into deep, hot fat. Makes about 6 servings.

HUSHPUPPIE

1 lb. water ground cornmeal
2 Tbsp. sugar
1 Tbsp. salt

1 egg, beaten
½ pint buttermilk pinch soda
¾ pint water

Combine all ingredients and mix well. Drop by spoonfuls into deep fat (375 degrees for fat). (Captain Bill uses Wesson oil.)

FRENCH BREAD DOUGH

2 ½ c. water (95 degrees) 2 Ib. 3 oz. bread flour, measured
2 pkgs. rapid-rise yeast,
dissolved in water

To mixing bowl add 4 cups flour to the water-yeast mixture. Mix with dough hook until it makes a sponge (pulls away from bowl). Add 2 teaspoons of salt that has dissolved in a little warm water. Then add rest of flour. (I cannot see that this needs this much flour… or add more water… I also add some Crisco to mixture.) Pour out onto formica or marble counter top. Knead a little, cover with bowl, let rise L hour. Punch down, cover, let rise another hour. Then punch down, knead, make into loaves. Put cornmeal on bottom of pan. Bake at 450°F for 24 minutes. Makes 3 or 4 small French type loaves. (Can use for other breads as basic recipe.)

EASY TO SHAPE AND BAKE VARIETY ROLLS

MONKEY BREAD - Use appx. 24 rolls (1 pkg.) & ¼ c. butter, melted. Cut each thawed roll in half. Dip each piece into melted butter; arrange pieces in layers in 9" ring mold. Allow dough to rise until it reaches top of pan (about 1 ½ to 2 hours.) Bake in 375°F oven 20-25 minutes or until golden brown. Variations: Garlic - add garlic powder to butter. Parmesan - dip dough pieces in parmesan cheese after butter.

BREAD STICKS - Stretch or roll each roll piece to desired length. Brush with melted butter. Place on lightly greased cookie sheet. Let rise appx. 15 minutes. Bake in 400°F oven for 10 minutes or until golden brown.

CINNAMON ROLLS - Dip rolls in melted butter. Roll in mixture of ½ c. sugar and 2 tsp. cinnamon per 1 dozen rolls. Place rolls in 9" cake pan or muffin tin. * After baking, glaze with mixture of ½ c. powdered sugar and 1 Tbsp. water.

HONEY NUT BUNS - Place 1 tsp. margarine or- butter, 1 Tbsp. honey and 2 tsp. chopped nuts in each cavity of muffin pan. Place dough on top. Brush with melted butter. *

ZEPPOLI - Tear each roll in half, stretch slightly. Deep fry in 375°F oil until golden brown. Drain on absorbent paper; serve sprinkled with powdered sugar, cinnamon sugar or honey.

FLAVORED ROLLS - Place rolls on cookie sheet, muffin pan or cake pan. Brush rolls with egg wash (1 egg mixed with 2 Tbsp. water). Sprinkle with minced onions, parmesan cheese, grated cheese, poppy, sesame, or caraway seeds. *

*Let rise until doubled in size. Bake in at 375°F for 12-15 minutes. Remove from pan immediately to cool.

RED'S SOUTHERN HOT ROLLS

Rotha

This recipe takes a little time and physical effort. Try this for the best rolls you can ever eat. If at first you don't succeed, try several more times. Bread is something that takes some understanding to handle. Also, you will have better luck with rolls on warm days because of the rising problem… The warmer the day, the better yeast will cooperate.

2 pkgs. Yeast
2 c. warm water (not hot, but warmer than luke warm)
5 tbsp. sugar
½ c. Crusco (measure carefully by floating Crico in a half cup water in measuring cup… When it hits full cup with Crisco, it's measured correctly.
¼ tsp. salt
4 heaping c. plain flour

Mix water, salt, sugar and Crisco in bowl until all is well dissolved. Use mixer to smooth well. Add flour at high speed with mixer or bread dough hooks.

In your large mixing bowl or bread bowl, give dough a good beating with your hand. (A rolling motion that will make the dough flop hard. Dough will become nearly unbeatable after about 12 to 15 times.)

Grease a huge bowl with Crisco and place dough in it and let it rise. Use pastry brush and brush top of dough with Crisco oil. Keep out of draft and cover with thin cloth. Dough should rise to twice its size. This will take about 45 minutes more or less, depending on warmth conditions.

Punch down dough and knead with plain flour until it is elastic-like. Lift dough to height of your raised arms and throw down hard… Do this 5 to 6 times. Don't ask why… Just do it… It does something to the rolls. I tried to get by without doing this 'throw down job' and my rolls were like shoe leather.

Grease your hands slightly and make rolls and place into pan. Let rise a second time. Spread melted margarine lightly over tops of rolls then bake at 425°F until plump and brown. Again spread with margarine lightly to keep from being crusty.

NOTE: I love to roll dough out thin (¼"). Generously spread butter over then roll into a long roll. Cut in 1 ½" pieces and place each in greased muffin tin; let rise. Bake at 475°F for approximately 8 minutes or until brown. While hot from the oven, brush butter on tops and cool 5 minutes. Dump onto towel. Cool 5 more minutes and cover up or place in plastic wrap.

Freezing cooked rolls works great. Brown less for this if possible and warm in toaster later.

RED'S NUT-CHEESE BISCUITS

Rotha

2 c. Red-Band flour, self-rising
1 c. buttermilk
½ c. Crisco
Mix above ingredients well and add:

½ c. shredded cheddar cheese, (lightly floured)
½ c. pecans, (lightly floured)

Knead 25 times. Roll dough to ¾ inch thickness. Cut out and bake for 15 minutes at 400 degrees. For variation try substituting cheese with chopped apples and pecans with walnuts.
Serve with fresh honey and butter.

BANANA NUT BREAD

1 stick butter
1 c. sugar
2 eggs
2 c. mashed, ripe bananas
2 c. plain flour

1 tsp. baking powder
1 tsp. soda
1 tsp salt
½ c. chopped pecans
½ c raisins

Cream butter and sugar, add eggs, beat well. Add bananas and mix until smooth. Combine flour and dry ingredients; add to creamed mixture stirring just enough to moisten. Stir in pecans and raisins. Bake in greased and floured loaf pan for 1 hour to 1 hour 10 minutes at 350 degrees. Makes 1 large loaf. Use 9 x 5 x 3-inch loaf pan or two small ones.

YEAST ROLLS

Rotha

1 c. med. warm water	1 tsp. salt
2 pkg. yeast (¼ oz.)	4 c. plain flour
⅓ c. sugar	⅓ c. Crisco shortening softened

In warm, thick and large bowl, place water. Sprinkle yeast in. Stir until dissolved. Stir in salt and sugar.

Use dough hook and add in flour until mixed well and forms into a good mix. Turn onto a bed of flour and knead for about 7 minutes or until a smooth ball. Place into a very large bowl that is heavily greased with Crisco. Cover dough with a coating of Crisco. Cover and place in warm place for about 1 to 1 ½ hours or until dough is about double or more in size. Punch dough down and form ball again. You can roll it if you wish. Form a ball and again let it rise same as before. Often, if I have chores to do, I take the dough with me and do the 'rising' on the run.

When dough rises again, get to a floured surface and knead until dough forms a nice ball. Throw it in the air and let it flop onto the counter. I usually take it about three feet over my head and throw it down on the counter about four times. This get the bubbles out and makes a softer outcome. Then again, form into a ball and roll it out into a square-ish flat, ¼" (pizza-like) crust. Pour 1 stick of melted Blue Bonnet margarine over this and spread evenly, leaving about one inch without at the farside of the dough.

Grease your finger and roll dough gently into a long roll. Stretch somewhat so it will make more rolls. Let rest about eight minutes while you grease liberally muffin tins with Crisco. Cut rolls in 1 ½ inch pieces and place on flat side in each tin. Yield: 2 dozen rolls

Again, let rise to double. Bake in 485°F oven for 8 minutes or until golden brown. Brush with butter in pan then pour onto clean towel to cool slightly. Cover in bowl with towel. Enjoy!

CRANBERRY NUT BREAD

2 c. plain flour
1 c. sugar
1 ½ tsp. baking powder
½ tsp soda
1 tsp. salt
1 egg, well beaten

¼ c. Crisco
¾ c. orange juice
1 Tbsp. grated orange rind
½ c. chopped nuts
1 ½ c. coarsely chopped cranberries

Sift together dry ingredients. Cut in shortening until mixture looks like cornmeal. Combine orange juice and grated rind; add eggs. Pour all at once into dry ingredients, mixing just enough to dampen. Fold in cranberries and nuts. Spoon into greased loaf pan. Bake 1 hour at 350 degrees.

POO'S LUNCHBOX CASSEROLE

1 ½ lb. browned hamburger, drained
1 c. uncooked white rice
1 can (10 oz.) cream of chicken soup
1 (8 oz.) pkg. sour cream
1 c. shredded cheddar cheese
1 c. milk
1 c. water
1 tsp. chili powder

Mix together soup, sour cream, water, milk and chili powder. Add hamburger, rice and cheese. Pour into a greased casserole dish. Cook covered at 350°F for 1 ½ hours or until bubbly.

*To reduce fat and calories, use fat free sour cream, low fat soup and fat free milk.

*OPTIONS: Add ¼ c. onion and 1 finely chopped jalapeno pepper for extra kick.

CORN PUDDING CASSEROLE

1 can whole kernel corn, undrained
1 can cream style corn
2 eggs, well beaten
1 (8 oz.) pkg. sour cream
1 box Jiffy corn muffin mix

Mix all ingredients well. Bake at 350°F for 1 hour.

VEGGIE RICE BAKE

4 c. cooked rice
¼ c. diced onions
½ c. diced carrots
¼ c. diced celery

2 pkts. Or cubes beef broth, dry
2 Tbsp. olive oil salt and pepper to taste

Sauté vegetables in olive oil over low heat for 10 minutes or until slightly tender. Drain. Add beef broth (dry). (If using cubes, crumble). Stir well. Add rice. Stir again. Bake in 350°F oven for 20 minutes or until heated through. (Broccoli may be substituted for celery.)

VEGETABLE MARINADE

12 oz. Shoepeg corn, drained
12 oz. peas, drained
12 oz. green beans, drained
1 c. celery, chopped
1 bunch green onion, sliced
1 sn, green pepper, chopped

1 sm. Jar pimentos, chopped
¾ c. cider vinegar
½ c. salad oil.
1 c. sugar
1 tsp. each salt and pepper

Mix together corn, peas, green beans, celery, onions, pepper and pimentos. Set aside, Mix together vinegar, salad oil, sugar, salt and pepper. Bring this mixture to a boil and let cool. Pour ever vegetables and mix. Cover and chill in refrigerator overnight.

BUTTERNUT SQUASH CASSEROLE

2 c. butternut squash, cooked and mashed
3 eggs, slightly beaten
6 Tbsp. melted butter
1 c. milk
¾ c. sugar
¼ c. honey
½ tsp. ginger
½ c. pecans, chopped
⅓ c. buttered cracker crumbs

Mix all ingredients. Spoon into greased baking dish. Bake at 350°F for 55 minutes.

CHICKEN CATATORIA

1 fryer, cut up
1 med, onion, chopped
1 bunch green onions, chopped
1 jar pimentoes, chopped

2 cans golden mushroom soup
1 can chicken broth
2 c. rice
2 cans water

Pour chicken broth and soup in glass casserole dish. Add onions, pimentoes and rice. Mix well. Lay chicken on top. Sprinkle with salt and pepper. Cover with foil. Bake at 350°F for 1 ½ hours. Remove foil and bake an additional 15 minutes. Remove from oven and serve.

SWEET POTATO CASSEROLE

3 c. sweet potatoes, mashed
1 c. sugar
½ tsp. salt
⅓ stick butter, melted
½ c. evaporated milk
2 eggs, beaten

Combine potatoes, sugar, salt, butter, milk and eggs. Turn into greased baking dish.

TOPPING:

1 c. brown sugar
⅓ c. flour
⅓ stick butter
1 c. pecans or walnuts, chopped

Blend well and sprinkle on top of casserole. Bake at 350°F for 40-45 minutes. Serve 6.

GRANDMA'S FRIED/BAKED VEGETABLES

Use either squash, zucchini, eggplant or onion

Slice into ¼ inch thicknesses and salt each side slightly. Dip in buttermilk. Roll into self-rising flour. Place on a greased bread sheet and bake each side-frying in oven. (Use enough oil!) Add margarine if desired. Pepper lightly white hot.

POTATO CASSEROLE

4 lg. baking potatoes

Wash, trim and cut potatoes in large hunks. Sprinkle with salt. Place in a medium, greased casserole dish.

1 ½ c. water   1 sm. Container sour cream
2 Tbsp. chopped, fresh parsley

Pour water over potatoes, sprinkle with parsley. Drop butter chunks over top. Bake in 375°F oven for approximately 40 minutes or until done when checked with fork. When ready to serve, pour a small container of sour cream over top. Do not stir. It will melt in.

½ stick butter, cut into small   Black pepper to taste
chunks

3 pkg. broccoli   1 (4 ½ oz.) jar mushrooms,
1 tube Kraft garlic cheese   drained, sliced
1 (3 oz.) pkg. cream cheese   1 can cream of mushroom soup
                                  ½ stick margarine

Cook broccoli according to package directions. Cut cheeses and margarine. Mix in mushrooms and soup. Butter your casserole dish. Layer broccoli and cheese mixture, ending with cheese mixture. Bake at 350°F for 40 minutes.

BRUNCH SAUSAGE CASSEROLE

1 Ib. pork sausage	4 eggs, beaten
1 can refrigerated crescent dinner rolls	¾ c. milk
	¼ tsp. salt
2 c. shredded Mozzorella cheese	⅛ tsp. pepper

Crumble sausage in skillet. Cook over medium heat until brown, stirring constantly. Drain well. Line bottom of buttered 13x9x2 inch baking dish with crescent rolls, pressing perforations to seal. Sprinkle with sausage and cheese. Combine remaining ingredients, beating well. Pour over sausage and cheese layer. Bake at 425°F for 15 minutes or until set. Let stand 5 minutes. Cut in squares and serve immediately. Yield: 6- 8 servings.

BREAKFAST CASSEROLE

1 pkg. (14 oz.) hot sausage
6 eggs
1 c. milk
6 slices bread, crumbled for bread crumbs
½ tsp. dry mustard
red crushed pepper, to taste
½ tsp. cayenne peeper
1 Tbsp. Texas Pete
1 c. shredded sharp cheddar cheese

Brown sausage, drain and set aside to cool. In a large bowl mix eggs and milk with a whisk. Add mustard and spices. Stir in bread crumbs, sausage and cheese. Spray a 13x9 baking dish with Pam. Pour mixture into dish. Let set overnight covered in refrigerator. Bake at 350°F for 20 to 30 minutes.

SCALLOPED POTATOES

Boil 5 or 6 medium potatoes in jackets (not too long or they will crumble). Cool, peel and cut into chunks or slices. Into a saucepan place.

1 sm. Can of milk	1 onion, chopped

Add:

Garlic powder	Parmesan cheese
Parsley flakes	1 pkg. American cheese slices

Melt over low heat. Pour over potatoes and bake until bubbly ad 350°F.

CABBAGE ROLL

Place cabbage in freezer over night to freeze. Remove from freezer and remove core. Separate leaves and place in a pot of boiling water. Boil until leaves are tender. Do not overcook.

Mix the following:

1 ½ lb. beef	1 tsp. salt
1 ½ c. rice, uncooked	1 Tbsp. Italian seasoning
2 eggs	1 tsp. garlic powder
¼ tsp. allspice	½ c. ketchup or tomato sauce,
½ tsp. pepper	(enough to turn mixture red)

Put mixture in cabbage leaves, roll up and secure with toothpicks.

Mix the following in a pot:

1 sin, jar Ragu	1 sm. can tomato
1 (6 oz.) can tomato sauce	paste or ketchup
	1 ½ c. water

Pour over cabbage and cover completely. Bring to a boil and cook for approximately L hour.

NOTE: You may substitute cabbage with halved bell peppers.

BEAN CASSEROLE

1 pkg. boiled hot dogs   1 lg. onion, chopped
1 lb. ground beef   1/s tsp. garlic

Brown together and drain. Pour into greased baking dish.

Combine;

2 tsp. dried mustard   1 lg. can pork & beans
⅓ c. brown sugar   1 can kidney beans
½ c. catsup   8 slices bacon

Pour over hamburger mixture in baking dish. Sprinkle top with bread crumbs and cheese. Top with slices of bacon. Bake, in oven for 30 minutes at 350°F.

GALE'S CHICKEN CASSEROLE

4 cans Swanson's chicken
2 ctn (1 pt. size) sour cream
1 can cream of chicken soup
1 can cream of celery soup
1 lg. can Swanson's chicken stock
2 pks Pepperidge Farm dressing mix
2 sticks margarine

Melt margarine and add to dressing mix. Line dish with half of the dressing, then chicken. Mix soup with sour cream. Pour over dressing and chicken layer. Top with remaining dressing. Pour chicken stock over all. Bake at 350°F for about 45 minutes or until hot.

SQUASH CASSEROLE

2 lb. (3 c.) squash, sliced
½ c. onion, chopped
¼ c. green pepper, chopped
½ c. bread crumbs
½ c. sour cream

½ c. cheese soup
½ c. water
1 Tbsp. corn starch
½ tsp. garlic powder
curry, if desired

Place squash, onion, green pepper and ¼ cup bread crumbs in a buttered baking dish. Combine sour cream, cheese soup, water, corn starch and garlic powder. Pour over squash layer. Sprinkle top with another ¼ cup of bread crumbs. Bake at 350°F for 30 to 40 minutes.

SWEET POTATO SOUFFLE

4 med. Sweet potatoes, cooked, peeled and mashed
½ c. can milk
½ stick margarine
½ c. sugar

1 egg, beaten
½ c. orange juice
1 tsp. or 1 orange rind, grated
Small amount cinnamon

While potatoes are still hot add milk, margarine and sugar. Mix in egg, orange juice, orange rind and cinnamon. Bake at 350°F for 25 minutes or until egg is cooked. Marshmallows may be placed on top during last 5 minutes of baking time.

CABBAGE CASSEROLE

½ head cabbage, cooked
1 can undiluted celery soup
1 sleeve Ritz crackers, crushed
¼ stick butter or margarine, melted
Grated cheddar cheese

Cook cabbage till done. Put into a greased casserole dish. Cover with celery soup. Sprinkle with a layer of cheddar cheese. Mix cracker crumbs with melted margarine. Top cheese with cracker crumbs. Bake at 350°F for 20 30 minutes until heated through. Good warmed over.

PEAS SUPREME

½ c. water
2 Tbsp. butter
2 c. celery
2 pkg frozen peas
1 can cream of mushroom soup warmed

1 sm. Can sliced mushrooms, or fresh
1 can water chestnuts
¾ c. bread crumbs
2 Tbsp. butter, melted

Combine water, butter, celery and frozen peas. Cook until tender 15 minutes on med-low heat. Place peas in buttered casserole dish. Layer peas with soup, mushrooms and chestnuts. Combine bread crumbs with melted butter. Place bread crumbs on top of casserole and bake at 350°F for 20 minutes.

ASPARAGUS CASSEROLE

(stove top)

1 can asparagus, drained
½ stick margarine, melted
1 can Vienna Sausages, drained and cut in half
1 egg

1 Tbsp. water
salt and pepper to taste
2 lg. slices Kraft Swiss cheese
slivered almonds

In a small frying pan combine asparagus, margarine and Vienna Sausages. Neatly arrange sausages with fingers. Beat egg and water. Pour over asparagus mixture. Salt and pepper to taste. Place cheese on top. Sprinkle with almonds and cover. Cook until egg is done at low eat on top of stove for approximately 8 minutes. Cut in fourths and serve with toast or rice muffins, applesauce and coffee.

ONION CASSEROLE

2 - 3 lg. onions, sliced
1 can cream of celery soup
2 cans cream of mushroom soup

2 - 3 c. cornflakes
1 stick butter, melted
salt and pepper

In an oblong Pyrex or Corning dish, place rows of sliced, large onions. (Slice the onions about ½ to ¾ inches thick and do not take the rings apart.) Salt and pepper to taste. Mix together the soups. Pour over the onions. Top with cornflakes. Drizzle melted butter over cornflakes. Bake at 350°F for 1 hour or until onions are tender. Do not overcook.

GALE'S CHICKEN PIE

1 (2 ½ - 3 Ib.) chicken
L stick butter
1 c. plain flour
3 tsp. baking powder
½ tsp. black pepper

1 tsp. salt
1 c. milk
1 can cream of celery soup
1 can chicken broth

Cook chicken till tender; pull from bones. Place in Pyrex dish. Melt butter; pour over chicken. Sift flour with baking powder, salt and pepper. Blend in milk till smooth. Spread mixture evenly over chicken. Blend soup and broth. Bring to boil; pour over flour mixture. Bake at 375°F to 400°F for 1 hour or until brown. (Don't throw away chicken broth—freeze it. If pie is left over, add more broth and heat again.)

CHICKEN-VEG SAUTE

4 chicken breasts, deboned, cleaned & cut into 1" square pieces
½ head cabbage, cut up
2 med. Squash, thinly sliced
6 fresh mushrooms, thick sliced
1 lg. onion, sliced

1 lg. onion, sliced
4 sticks celery, cut up
Large pinch dried mint
Large pinch anise seed
Salt to taste
¼ c. vegetable oil

In aluminum pan pour in vegetable oil. Heat; put in chicken bits. Fry or saute for about 6 minutes or until near done. Pour off fat. Add mint, anise, celery and onion. Cook 2 more minutes, covered. Add rest of vegetables; saute for 3 to 4 minutes covered. Stir vegetables and meat occasionally. Serve over rice with fruit salad on the side.

DEBONED CHICKEN CASSEROLE

8 deboned chicken breasts, halved lean bacon strips
1 lg. jar dried beef slices
2 cans cream of mushroom soup
1 pt. sour cream
1 can cream of chicken soup

Wrap each piece of chicken with lean bacon. Line casserole dish or pan with dried beef slices. Mix together soups and sour cream. Pour over the chicken. Cover dish tightly with foil and bake at 350°F for one hour then 1 to 2 hours at 325°F (till chicken is tender and soups bubbly). This is much better when baked ahead of time and warmed up. I make this and freeze for future use. Serve over rice.

CHELIES RELLENOS

(Stuffed Chilies)

2 (4 oz.) cans whole green chilies
1 (10 oz.) can tomatoes & green chilies
½ Ib. cheddar cheese
flour for coating
2 eggs, separated
½ tsp. salt
Shortening

Stuff chilies with strips of cheese. Coat generously with flour. Beat egg whites until stiff. Beat egg yolks and fold in beaten egg whites; add salt. Dip stuffed chilies into egg mixture. Fry in hot shortening until golden brown on both sides. Serve immediately with heated tomatoes and green chilies, spooned over top to add zesty flavor.

SASSY LADY'S OYSTERS IN A CASSEROLE

2 containers (12 oz. ea.) medium-size fresh oysters
1 can chicken broth
1 sm. Onion, finely chopped
½ tsp. paprika
1 tsp. salt
1 tsp. black pepper
¾ tsp. garlic powder
1 tsp. Worcestershire sauce
juice of 1 lemon
½ c. butter or margarine
½ c. plain flour
1 c. cracker crumb

In a large saucepan, cook oysters in their own juice until edges curl. Remove oysters with a slotted spoon. Set aside.

Using all oyster liquid combine with chicken broth to equal 1 & ½ cups. To mixed liquid add all seasoning ingredients.

In a separate pan, melt butter. Stir in flour, cook over medium heat about 2 ½ minutes, stirring constantly, until mixtures turns golden brown. Remove from heat.

Slowly stir oyster liquid into flour mixture. In a 1 ½-quart baking dish lay oysters in bottom and pour in sauce mixture. Sprinkle cracker crumbs evenly over top. Bake at 390°F for 25 minutes.

STUFFED FERRARA

Rotha

(Read the entire recipe before beginning)

12 oz. box jumbo shells   2 Tbsp. Crisco oil

Boil shells in large pot of salted water with Crisco oil. Do not overcook. Pour into large colander and run cool water over these. Gently hand wash. Keep wet until ready to stuff. When ready to stuff drain and pick up one at a time.

SAUCE

2 ½ lb. lean ground beef   1 Tbsp. seeds from green pepper
1 tsp. salt   1 Tbsp. paprika
2 Tbsp. dry, coarse garlic   1 Tbsp. coarse crushed
2 Tbsp. oregano   red pepper or
1 med. onion, chopped   1 can cherry pepper
1 med. green pepper, chopped

Brown ground beef with salt, garlic, oregano, onion, green pepper, pepper seeds, paprika and red pepper. When this is done reserve ⅓ of mixture fox the sauce Leave this ⅓ in the big pot and add:

1 lg. jar Ragu sauce   1 c. catsup
1 lg. can tomato sauce   1 sm. can tomato paste

If you like, use 8 large Italian sausage links that have been boiled in water until done. Pour off water, brown in 2 tsp. margarine. Set aside. Cut into pieces before adding to sauce. You do not have to use the Italian sausage.

STUFFING: Mix in large mixing bowl the following:

⅔ meat mixture (from sauce)	1 pkg. Kraft mild cheddar cheese, grated
1 pkg. Kraft med. sharp cheddar cheese, grated	8 oz. pkg. cream cheese
	8 oz. pkg. Kraft American cheese

Liberally grease a large baking, dish with margarine. Spoon in a small amount of sauce into bottom of dish. Take each shell and stuff a large amount of the stuffing mix inside. Place on top of sauce. When layer is done add sauce over this. Continue with stuffed shells until all stuffing is gone. Pour remaining sauce over all. Sprinkle parmesan cheese liberally over the, top of casserole. Bake 30 minutes at 375°F (not in microwave.

NOODLES

Cook small package flat egg noodles to near done; be sure and salt once boiling. Pour off water in collander and wash.

Saute:

½ stick margarine ½ green pepper, chopped
5 green onions, chopped ½ c. fresh parsley, chopped
2 celery stalks, chopped

Add:

big dash Worcestershire sauce 1 can kidney beans, drained

Return noodles to pot and heat. Stir in ½ c. sour cream. Serves 4 (or 2 hogs!)

PART 2

RIB ROASTS

For cooking large rib roasts, 4 ribs or larger, to cook a medium-rare roast: Preheat oven to 500°F. Place roast on a rack in a roasting pan and put in oven. Roast for 45 minutes; turn off heat. Do not open the door. Leave the roast in the oven an additional two hours and it's ready to serve.

FRENCH MEAT LOAF

1 ½ lb. lean ground beef
1 pkg. Waverly crackers, crushed fine
2 eggs, beaten lightly
1 ½ tsp. salt
1 med. onion chopped
½ c. ketchup
1 Tbsp. Worcestershire sauce
¾ can cheddar cheese soup
½ c. water
1 Tbsp. poppy seed
½ Tbsp. cumin seed

Mix beef, cracker crumbs, eggs, salt, onion, ketchup and Worcestershire sauce well. Butter an 8x8x½-inch pan or Pyrex dish. Place meat loaf in pan; punch around in meat loaf with fingers to indent lots of 'holes.' Mix soup with water; pour over meat loaf. Sprinkle with poppy and cumin seed. Cover; bake at 350°F for 1 ½ hours; pour off extra sauce. Brown at 450°F (about 10 to 20 minutes). Serve.

STEAK MARINATED

Rotha

1 thick sirlon tip steak,
1 or 2 inches thick
⅔ c. dry wine
1 Tbsp. soy sauce
⅛ tsp. oregano

2 Tbsp. parsley flakes
⅛ tsp. black pepper
juice of ½ lemon
1 Tbsp. sugar

Use fork, and punch into steak to tenderize. Mix together wine, soy sauce, oregano. parsley, pepper, lemon juice and sugar. Place meat in long glass baking dish and pour marinade mix over it. Cover and chill over night or 12 hours, turning meat once or twice.

Ready the charcoal and place meat on grill when ready. (Meat should be dried with paper towels.) Broil each side about 5 to 7 minutes, according to doneness you prefer.

Slice thin on a diagonal-cross grain to serve. Serve with rice and fresh, fruit salad.

MY LONDON BROIL

London Broil	Salt, pepper, garlic powder
Meat tenderizer	1 tsp. ground mustard dash
½ c. oil	Worcestershire sauce
⅓ c. vinegar	Seasoning salt, opt.

Sprinkle meat with meat tenderizer on both sides. Prepare marinade over heat. Pour marinade over meat. Let stand for several hours or overnight in refrigerator. Cook as desired, or 400 degrees' oven for 1 hour

PORK TENDERLOIN IN GRAVY

8 to 12 pork tenderloin slices, ¼ inch thick
Salt and pepper
Flour
Crisco

1 lg onion, chopped
1 sm. Green pepper, chopped
3 sticks celery, diced
3 Tbsp. corn starch
2 c. warm water

Beat the heck out of the tenderloin. Salt and pepper to taste. Roll in flour and place in fast frying Crisco. Brown on both sides. (Don't let over heat.) Add onion, green pepper and celery to pan and cook slightly. Mix together the corn starch and warm water. Stir into pan with meat and onion mixture. Blend quickly and be ready to add additional water to thin as needed or desired. Salt gravy to taste. Let simmer for 5 minutes or so, stirring constantly.

This is a fast meal. Can serve with rice, noodles or potatoes.

CREAMED PEPPER STEAK

Rotha

Serve over rice. Prepare your favorite rice as directed. Time the rice to finish with the pepper steak to serve steaming hot.

2 lb. tender strips of filet or sirlon of beef	½ sm. can cooked mushrooms, drained
1 sm. onion, sliced	2 lg. green peppers, chopped
¼ c. corn oil	salt and pepper to taste
2 Tbsp. olive oil	1 c. skim milk
	3 Tbsp. flour

Heat electric fry pan with the butter at 400°F. Salt and pepper steak, roll in flour and fry rapidly with the onion, peppers and mushrooms. When meat is browned well on both sides, Mix ½ cup milk with flour (it should be quite watery). Pour into the frying pan and mix well and fast. Add and mix the other ½ cup of milk. Reduce heat to 300°F for 5 minutes. Let simmer at 250°F for 10 minutes. Keep warm until ready to serve.

ROAST PORK OR LAMB WITH FRUIT SAUCE

Rotha

4 slices pineapple, drained
1 (16 oz.) can apricots, drained
1 (16 oz.) can peaches, drained
3 Tbsp. butter
3 Tbsp. brown sugar
⅛ tsp. cinnamon
⅛ tsp. cloves
juice of ½ lemon
2 tsp. white vinegar

Wrap meat in foil; put in preheated 475°F oven. (Cooking time should be 25 minutes per pound.) When roast is 45 min. from being done, prepare sauce. Combine fruits butter, sugar, cinnamon, cloves, lemon juice and vinegar in blender. Pour sauce over roast; finish cooking. Serve with rice. Use the fruit sauce as a pour-on gravy.

EARLY BIRD'S LAMB CHOPS

Rotha

12 lamb chops
salt
pepper
1 med. onion, chopped fine

1 lb. sliced mushrooms
½ stick. butter melted
½ c. water

Salt lamb chops to taste. Grill (charcoal best) both sides to ½ done. Place in baking dish, peppering one side generously. Scatter over top the chopped onions, sliced mushrooms, butter and water. Cover tight and bake at 475°F for approximately 15 minutes or until everything blends together. Serve with peach chutney. This will drive you crazy! You'll crave it forever.

RED'S LAMB WITH SAUCE

Rotha

1 leg of lamb (10 lb. or so)   2 c. water
salt and pepper   1 onion, chopped.

Place leg of lamb in foil lined iron frying pan using sheets long enough to wrap top securely. Add water and onion; cover securely. Bake in 475°F oven at 22 minutes per pound.

When 30 minutes from being done pour off most of the water, Pour prepared sauce and finish baking.

SAUCE

1 sm. can peaches   juice of 1 lemon
1 sm. can apricots   juice of 1 orange
1 apple, chopped   ½ c. brown sugar

Put all ingredients in blender mix. Fruit should be coarse.

GREENLAKE PORK TENDERLOIN CURRY

Rotha

2 lb. pork tenderloin, cut into 1 ½ inch chunks
cooked rice
1 stick butter, cut in half
¼ c. Crisco oil
1 sm. onion.
garlic powder
salt and ground pepper
½ - 1 tsp. curry powder, opt.
1 lb. frozen green peas
½ green pepper
½ lb. halved fresh mushrooms

Prepare rice and green peas together. Drain and have ready when meat is cooked. Salt to taste before cooking; remember to add slightly more salt for the peas but use the rice directions on the package of rice. To sauté pork, combine ½ stick butter, Crisco oil and meat. Brown slowly (medium heat) about 8 minutes. Add salt, garlic and ground pepper to taste. Swirl together flipping the flavors together. Add onion, green pepper and mushrooms. Mix well. Sauté for 3 minutes on medium heat.

Remove all ingredients from pan now; set aside, keeping hot.

Now put the rice and peas into the sauté pan; add the rest of the butter and curry powder. Fry slightly on medium heat about 6 minutes; do not let it burn. Return the meat mixture to the sauté pan with the rice and peas. Very slightly and carefully, stir together. Serve in individual casserole dishes, piping hot. Have prepared chilled pineapple (fresh if possible) and strawberries or cherries for color. Sprinkle lightly with powdered sugar.

CORNED BEEF EYRES PLACE

Rotha

3 - 4 lb. Kosher corned beef
1 lg. carrot
1 lg. onion
2 lg. celery stalks
10 black peppercorns
1 tsp. garlic powder or chopped garlic
½ tsp. dry mustard
1 tsp. salt, or to taste
1 can beef broth

Place all ingredients in large roaster. Cover with hot water. Stir slightly and bring to full boil for 20 minutes. Reduce to a medium boil and cover (not tightly). Cook for approximately 2 hours. Check occasionally and add water as needed, keeping to a boil. Do not let beef boil dry. Add beef broth and 1 c. water at this point. Reduce to a lower simmer; cover tightly and cook about 1 ½ hours longer. Serve with cabbage, new potatoes and carrots.

HOW TO DEBONE A CHICKEN BREAST

    a.   Purchase number of breasts desired
    b.   Wash in cold water with 1 Tbsp. Clorox. Rinse.
    c.   Remove skin and undersirable fat
    d.   Put chicken breast on fat surface, breast bone down, (chopping block is okay). Split breast bone with knife
    e.   Take finger and slip it between the bone and meat. Slowly separate.
    f.   Use the bones for soup if desired. The meat is ready for its need.

EXOTIC BEEF STROGANOFF

Rotha

2 lb. beef tenderloin, thinly sliced	¾ c. water
1 onion, very small	½ c. milk
1 sm. can sliced mushrooms	½ stick margarine
2 Tbsp. flour	1 sm. pkg. egg noodles
¾ c. water	2 Tbsp. light, dry rum
½ c. milk	salt and pepper
8 oz. sour cream	2 sm. Irish potatoes

Boil noodles while working on the beef. In electric fry pan, melt margarine. Add beef and let simmer at 300°F. Salt beef to taste. Meanwhile, peel and slice potatoes; boil until well done. When thoroughly cooked, pour off most of water, making a thick soup. Salt to taste.

When beef is ¼ done add pepper to taste, diced onion and a touch of garlic powder if desired. Add water from mushrooms when beef is ½ or medium done. Add potatoes and mushrooms. (Don't forget to have the noodles cooking!)

Add rum.

Take flour and mix until smooth with ¾ c. water. Four into frying pan and mix well. Now, slowly mix in the milk and sour cream. Let simmer at 300°F until noodles are ready. You may add noodles into mixture or serve stroganoff on top of noodles. Dinner is. served!

This whole process is easy and a tasteful delight. On not so special days or for unexpected company try this with hamburger meat, treating your guests with a special surprise.

EASTON, WA. BARBECUED PORK CHOPS

Rotha

2 lb. thinly sliced, center cut pork chops
1 stick butter
¼ c. Crisco
¼ tsp. dried chili pepper flakes
1 Tbsp. sugar
1 lg. bottle tomato sauce
juice of 2. lemons
2 Tbsp. vinegar
½ tsp. allspice

Heat electric frying pan. Melt butter. Salt and pepper pork chops and place in pan, frying fast but not letting the butter burn. Fry chops well-done. Pour in lemon juice, tomato sauce, and vinegar. Add chili pepper flakes and sugar. Reduce heat to 250°F and let simmer for 20 to 30 minutes. Serves 4.

CHICKEN AND CHEESE SAUCE

Rotha

3 ½ lb. fryer
2 c. cornflakes
2 eggs
½ c. milk
salt and pepper

Prepare chicken to cook. Beat egg and water to a foam. Mash cornflakes slightly. Dip chicken pieces into egg then roll carefully in cornflakes. Place on foil lined cookie sheet and place into 425°F oven for about 45 minutes or until done. Uses Magic Sauce recipe from Salmon, Elliot Bay, BUT LEAVE OUT lemon juice and shrimp meat and add more cheese. and mushrooms as desired.

BARBECUED CHICKEN OR RIBS

Clean and season 3 ½ lb. fryer chicken and/or 3 lb. ribs. Salt and pepper as desired. Charcoal broil or broil meat for about 20 to 28 minutes, turning continually. Allow to cook through, but don't cook dry.

Prepare sauce:

1 (16 oz.) bottle ketchup	3 Tbsp. sugar
½ stick butter	6 Tbsp. white vinegar
juice of 1 lemon	½ c. water

Place all of the above ingredients in a sauce pan and bring to a boil. Reduce heat to slow simmer. Allow to simmer while meat cooks. When meat is done, remove it to a foil lined casserole. dish and pour sauce over slowly and be certain to spread it over all pieces evenly. Place into a preheated 450°F oven for. 20 minutes. Do not cover. Remove from foil to serving dish immediately.

SASSY LADY'S EASY CHICKEN

Select chicken breast (4 to 8 depends on family size).

Remove fat and skin wash well then dry with towel.

Salt to taste.

Place ¼ c. Crisco oil in heavy skillet. Heat to frying temperature and place chicken in oil. Cook on med-high heat for about 30 minutes. Allow meat to get golden brown, turning occasionally.

Sprinkle paprika and dried parsley flakes generously over chicken when it is half done.

When meat is done, pour off all extra oil from bottom of pan.

Pour off liquid of 1 lg. can peach halves. Take ½ c. liquid and add to chicken. Slip peach halves into pan. Sprinkle ¼ c. lt. brown sugar over peaches, a little cinnamon and ¼ c. slivered almonds.

Add 1 heaping tsp. corn starch to ¼ c. water. Pour in and stir well. As it thickens add more water if desired for thinner gravy.

Place on platter surrounding with peach, halves and gravy over chicken.

CHICKEN AND SAUCE

4 chicken breast halves
salt & pepper to taste
¼ c. Crisco oil
2 Tbsp. mayonnaise
½ tsp. corn starch
1 ½ c. water
rice
green peas

Remove skin and fat from chicken. Salt & pepper to taste. Place in Crisco oil; saute until done (covered). Pour off fat. Combine the mayonnaise, corn starch and water. Pour over chicken, stirring lightly while turning chicken, making a gravy. Serve with rice and green peas.

*This is fast to prepare. It takes only 10 to 15 minutes. Prepare rice as directed. Warm green peas. Have rice and peas ready the same time chicken is done.

MAGIC SAUCE

Rotha

Ready your double boiler. When water boils, reduce heat to slow boil. Place 3 Tbsp. butter in top of boiler pan. Allow it to melt.

Add 3 Tbsp. flour. Blend until smooth. (Use wooden spoon.)

Add 1 ½ c. milk and stir constantly. Cook until thick and smooth, about 5 minutes.

Add:

½ tsp. salt	½ lb. grated sharp
juice from ½ lemon (more	cheddar cheese
if you prefer more tart)	½ c. shrimp meat
1 c. lg. mushrooms, thinly sliced	¼ tsp. parsley

Stir for 1 minute to help blend together then cover and let simmer very slowly about 5 minutes. Set aside. until time to serve. Will serve 4 to 6 people.
When salmon is ready, place on individual plates or on a platter with sauce poured over it.

SALMON FOR TWO

1 (5 oz.) pkg. egg noodles
small amount chopped onion
½ c. sour cream
2 to 4 tsp milk

1 (7 ¾ oz.) can
salmon, drained & flaked
½ tsp. parsley flakes

Cook noodles according to package directions. Add onion, sour cream, salmon, parsley and milk. Bake in a 1 qt. casserole dish at 350°F for 30 minutes or until bubbly.

SALMON, ELLIOT BAY

(To be topped with MAGIC SAUCE)

Rotha

2 ½ lb. salmon
salt
6 thin butter patties

3 lg. pinches dry parsley
½ c. water
½ c. milk

Clean and bone fish—do not remove skin but do remove the scales. Line bottom of large frying pan with aluminum foil; be sure of having a cover that will fit. Place six thin patties of butter in bottom of pan. Salt gently and place salmon (skin side down) in pan. Mix together water and milk; pour over salmon. Sprinkle with parsley. Cover tightly and cook over low heat for 20 minutes or until tender.

Do not overcook. Salmon is best cooked just before serving, from the pan to the table.

BROILED CRABS

2 Tbsp lemon juice
2 Tbsp. olive oil
1 Tbsp soy sauce
3 Tbsp. chopped fresh parsley
1 tsp. dried oregano

5 cloves garlic, minced
2 Tbsp. white wine
12 live hard-shell blue-claw crabs
7 Tbsp. flavored bred crumbs

In a large bowl, mix together lemon juice, olive oil, soy sauce, parsley, oregano, garlic and white wine. The night before crabs are to be cooked, place them in a paper bag and refrigerate overnight. (This numbs the crabs.) To cook them, remove their claws; pull off their backs and clean the crab bodies thoroughly by rinsing them under cold, running water. Place crabs in the bowl and let them marinate for 1 hour. Lay crabs right side up in a baking pan. Sprinkle them with the bread crumbs and pour in remaining marinating liquid. Broil crabs 6 to 8 inches from the heat until the shells turn red and the bread crumbs are brown, about 15 to 20 minutes. (Watch as they don't burn.). Makes 6 to 8 servings.

BAKED OYSTERS

Clean oysters in their shell. Place into 500°F oven for 14 minutes. Remove and serve in shell.

OYSTERS BATTERED

Rotha

1 c. pancake mix   lightly salted oysters
1 sm. Beer

Make a medium thin batter of pancake mix and beer. Dip salted oysters in batter. Deep fry. Cook at medium high heat (or about 8 minutes or until golden brown. (Same batter may be used for cooking fish, scallops, mushrooms., etc.)

LOU'S ALBECORE

1 lb. Albecore (fresh tuna)
1 onion, sliced thick
½ sm. green pepper, sliced thin
1 pkg. frozen spinach

¼ c. peanuts
8 fresh mushrooms, cleaned
¼ stick margarine
2 Tbsp. safflower oil

Place Albecore, onion, green pepper, spinach, peanuts, mushrooms and margarine in sauté pan. Stir fry for 8 minutes. (Remove. mushrooms last 2 minutes.) Serve with white rice and fresh tomato.

FRENCH CRAB LEGS OR SHRIMP

Rotha

½ lb. butter, melted
1 diced small onion, or
½ lb. sliced clean mushrooms, slightly salted

5 oz. butter, melted
Pre-cooked crab legs

Sweat mushrooms in melted butter for 2 minutes, uncovered. Add crab legs (pre-cooked) and heat. Stir in wine. Heat. Add and blend Fish Flavored White Sauce as base. Serve over rice mound with baby carrots.

FISH FLAVORED WHITE SAUCE

Rotha

1 lb. fish bones
carrots
celery
parsley
salt to taste

1 qt. water
4 oz. white dry wine
2 Tbsp. butter, melted
2 Tbsp. flour

Cook the fish bones, carrots celery, parsley and salt to the water and wine. Add butter and flour. Simmer to desired thickness.

SEA BASS SUPREME

6 Sea Bass (or Crappie) filets
juice of 1 ½ lemons
3 Tbsp. fresh dill
1 stick butter, softened
3 Tbsp. mayonnaise
2. Tbsp. sour cream
juice of 1 ½ lemons

4 cloves garlic, chop
1 c. parmesan cheese
2 spring onions
2 Tbsp. fresh dill
salt and pepper
seasoned bread crumbs

Combine juice of 1 ½. lemons and 3 Tbsp. fresh dill. Add fish filets and marinate. Mix well together the butter, mayonnaise, sour cream, juice of 1 ½ lemons, garlic, parmesan cheese, onions, dill weed, salt and pepper. Dip fish in this mixture, covering all sides. Carefully roll into seasoned bread crumbs. Bake at 375°F for 45 minutes.

FISH SAUTE

Rotha

½ lb. scallops
½ lb. halibut
½ lb. turbot
½ lb. fresh mushrooms, cleaned and clipped
1 stick celery
1 sm. onion, sliced thin and cut in half

½ c. corn oil
1 Tbsp. parsley
½ tsp. garlic powder or juice
½ c. lemon juice salt, if desired
1 c. sour cream, or ½ c. water with mushroom & 1 Tbsp. corn starch

Clean and dice scallops, halibut and turbot into 1 ½ inch squares. Ready fry pan with corn oil. Saute celery and onion for 2 minutes. Place meat in carefully. Add parsley and garlic. Saute until near done (5 to 7 minutes.) Add lemon/sour cream or water mixture and mushrooms last. Cover for 3 minutes, using an egg timer. Serve with noodles or rice.

BUTTER MILK FISH FILLETS

Rotha

2 lb. fish fillets
1 c. buttermilk
juice of 1 lemon
Crisco for deep frying

1 c. buttermilk pancake mix
2 tsp. salt
lemon wedges, opt.
malt vinegar, opt.

Place fish in a shallow baking dish. Pour buttermilk & lemon over fish; let stand 30 min., turning once. Combine pancake mix & salt. Remove fish from buttermilk; roll in dry mixture. Deep fry 3 to 4 min. or until brown. Drain on paper towels. (Can be fried in a skillet, turning to brown both sides.)

MT. RAINIER BEER BATTERED FISH

1 ½ lb. Crisco
½ c. bacon drippings & oil
1 sm. Onion

2 lb. fish
1 c. buttermilk pancake mix
½ can clear beer

Heat deep skillet with Crisco, bacon grease and drippings. Saute onion to flavor the heated oils; remove, keeping oil at a med-high heat for frying the fish. (Be careful not to let oil burn.) Clean and cut fish to your liking. Salt generously; set aside. Combine pancake mix and beer in large bowl making a fairly thin batter. Dip fish into batter; deep fry until brown. Serve hot or cold—a great party snack as well as a main dish.

CAPTAINS SEAFOOD DELIGHT

Rotha

¼ lb. shrimp
¼ lb. halibut
½ lb. oysters
¼ lb. turbot
¼ lb. salmon
¼ lb. squid
juice of 1 lemon
1 egg, beaten

1 onion, chopped
salt
1 onion, chopped
½ stick butter
1 ½ c. mayo
1 Tbsp. horseradish
½ c. pickle, chopped fine
½ pt. sour cream

Salt all fish. Dip in beaten egg. Saute in oil with onion. Remove fish as they brown to doneness. After all is cooked return to pan. Add butter, mayonnaise, horseradish, pickle and sour cream. Blend together until hot. Serve in individual dishes. Excellent with French Fries.

ROTHA'S BASIC PIE CRUST

(9" to 10")

2 ¼ c. plain flour
¼ tsp. salt
¼ tsp. sugar
¼ tsp. soda
½ c. + 1 Tbsp. Crisco
8 to 12 Tbsp. iced water

Sift together flour, sugar and soda. Blend Crisco in with a fork until dough has a bunch of tiny 'marbles' (Mixture will be slightly off-white in color and flakly-like). Spread water over this mixture then stir enough to hold it together. Make into one round ball with your hands. Crust will have a hollow-like sound and look a little splotchy. Put ball on wax paper and place in freezer for 8 minutes. Split dough in half to make two crusts. Use plenty of plain flour and roll out. Turnover, over and over, rolling constantly to get nice texture. Don't break crust. Place in butter greased pie pan, plate or can use for deep dish. This makes 3 or 4 crusts or one crust is used for top strips or crust is needed. Good for any pie!

GRAHAM CRACKER PIE SHELL

1 ½ c. fine graham cracker crumbs
½ c. melted butter
¼ c. sugar

Combine all ingredients and press into pie plate.

BING CHERRY PIE DELIGHT

1 sm. can cherries, drained, reserving juice
¼ c. walnuts, chopped
juice of ½ lemon
1 Tbsp. corn starch
¼ c. sugar
¼ c. cherry juice
¼ tsp. cinnamon
¼ tsp. almond flavoring

Combine lemon juice, corn starch, sugar, cherry juice, cinnamon and almond. Add cherries and walnuts. Turn into pie shell. Use pastry strips on top dot with butter. Bake at 375°F for 25 to 35 minutes.

APPLE-NUT PIE

6 - 8 Delicious apples
juice of 1 lemon
1 Tbsp. lemon jello
1 Tbsp. plain flour
¼ tsp. cinnamon

¼ C. pecans, chopped
1 ½ c. sugar
½ stick butter
¼ c. water, if needed

Clean, core and slice apples. Add all ingredients, except butter and water. Stir together until sugar dissolves. Add water if it is needed for more moisture. Place into pie. shell. Chip up butter and spread evenly. Roll out top crust; place on top of apples. Finish edge and make air-holes in top crust. Bake for 50 minutes (until brown) at 350°F.

BUTTERMILK PIE

1 c. sugar
½ stick butter
2 eggs, separated
2 Tbsp. buttermilk
1 tsp. lemon extract

Cream butter and sugar; add egg yolks, beating gently. Beat egg whites barely stiff. Add buttermilk and lemon juice to sugar mixture. Add beaten egg whites last. Stir gently; pour into 1 unbaked pie shell. Bake at 350°F for 25 to 30 minutes until set and firm.

PUMPKIN-ALMOND FLUFF PIE

Rotha

1 sm. can pumpkin
1 egg, slightly beaten
2 Tbsp. flour
½ tsp. almond flavoring
½ tsp. cinnamon

¼ c. brown sugar
¼ c. granulated sugar
¼ c. slivered almonds
2 Tbsp. butter

Mix all ingredients except almonds and butter. Pour into an 8" pie shell (unbaked). Dot shell with butter. Sprinkle almonds on top of pie and dot with rest of butter. Bake at 350°F to 360°F for about 30 minutes or until crust is browned nicely. (Makes one 8" pie.)

TEXAS PECAN PIE

5 eggs
3 Tbsp. butter, soft or melted
½ c. white sugar
1 ¼ c. white corn syrup
1 tsp. vanilla

3 Tbsp. flour
¼. tsp. salt
2 c. pecan halves
1 unbaked 9 or 10-inch pie shell

Beat eggs lightly. Add butter, sugar, syrup, vanilla, salt, flour and pecans. Pour into pie shell. Will be full. Bake at 350°F for about 45 minutes or until center is soft but not quite set.

SOUTHERN PECAN PIE

3 eggs, beaten
⅔ c. sugar
dash of salt

1 c. dark corn syrup
⅓ c. margarine, melted
1 c. pecan halves

Beat eggs thoroughly with sugar, salt, dark corn syrup and margarine. Add pecan halves. Pour into a 9-inch unbaked pastry shell. Bake at 350°F for 50 minutes.

ROCKY ROAD PIE

1 ½ c. cold half and half
1 sm. pkg. Jello chocolate or chocolate fudge instant pudding
8 oz. Cool Whip
½ c. Bakers semi-sweet chocolate chips
⅓ c. small marshmallows
⅓ c. chopped nuts
1 graham cracker pie crust

Pour half and half into large bowl. Add pudding mix. Beat with wire whisk until well blended. Let stand for 5 minutes. Fold in whipped topping, chocolate chips, marshmallows and nuts. Spoon into crust. Freeze until firm, 6 hours or overnight. Remove from freezer and let stand for 10 minutes to soften before serving. Store leftovers in freezer.

RHUBARB-TART PIE

Rotha

2 c. chopped rhubarb
½ apple, sliced thin
juice of ½ lemon
½ c. sugar
½ tsp. almond flavoring

¼ c. water
1 Tbsp. corn starch
1 tsp. flour
2 Tbsp. butter, melted

Combine all ingredients. (Be careful that corn starch not left lumpy.) Place in 8-inch pie shell. Cover top with strips of dough; dot with butter. Bake at 375°F for 35 minutes.

CUSTARD PIE

Rotha

1 c. sugar
½ stick butter, melted
2 eggs

1 c. milk
1 tsp coconut flavoring
2 Tbsp. all-purpose flour

Cream together sugar and butter. Add remaining ingredients and blend well (in listed order). Bake approximately 45 minutes at 360°F or until crust is done.

Note: For COCONUT PIE add 8 oz. pkg. frozen or fresh shredded coconut.

GERMAN CHOCOLATE PIE add ⅓ pkg. Baker's German chocolate squares and 1 c. chopped nuts and 1 more egg.

PECAN PIE add 1 c. finely chopped pecans. Stir in then scatter pecan halves on top of pie.

SOUR CREAM PIE

¾ c. white sugar
1 c. sour cream
2 eggs
2 Tbsp. flour

1 tsp. vanilla
½ c. chopped raisins
½ c. chopped pecans

Combine all ingredients and pour into an unbaked pie shell. Bake at 350°F till center sets, about 45 minutes. (Pie shell may be baked at 400°F for 5 minutes before pouring in filling.

BEST BUTTERNUT PIE

1 ½ c. butternut squash
1 c. brown sugar, (don't pack)
3 Tbsp. margarine
¼ tsp. cinnamon
½ tsp. almond flavoring

1 egg yolk
2 egg whites, beaten to peaks
¾ c. evaporated milk
¼ c. water
1 unbaked pie shell

Cut, peel and cook squash until soft enough to mash. Salt squash to taste, while boiling. When squash is done, pour off all water and let cool until cold. I often cook mine a day ahead or freeze for use later at this point. Combine all ingredients except egg whites; blend well. Stir in egg whites until smooth. Pour into pie shell; bake at 500°F for 8 minutes; reduce heat to 350°F for another 25-30 minutes.

COCONUT PIE

1 unbaked pie shell
4 eggs, well beaten
1 stick margarine, melted
1 c. sugar
1 ½ c. evaporated milk, diluted

½ c. regular milk
½ tsp. vanilla flavoring
½ tsp. coconut flavoring
1 c. flaked coconut

Mix well together the eggs, margarine, sugar, both milks, vanilla and coconut flavoring. Pour into unbaked pie shell. Sprinkle flaked coconut on top. Bake for 35 to 45 minutes in 350°F oven or until custard is firm.

PERFECT EGG CUSTARD

Rotha

4 eggs, beaten well
¾ c. sugar
2 c. cold milk
1 tsp. vanilla
⅛ tsp. salt

Beat eggs and sugar together. Add milk, vanilla and salt; beat again. Bake at 450°F for 5 minutes. Turn down oven to 250°F and bake for 45 minutes or more until firm. Use in pie shell or custard cups with metal or paper cups. Cook 5 minutes; turn oven down to 250°F. Bake 20 minutes or until firm. (Can cook on burner slowly until firm and pour in cups or crust.)

FRESH STRAWBERRY PIE

Rotha

1 qt. strawberries　　　1 ¼ c. sugar, (less if desired)
juice from 1 lemon　　　1 Tbsp. strawberry jello

Clean strawberries and cut in half. Mix lemon juice, sugar and jello with strawberries. Stir carefully so as not to break up berries yet enough to bring out enough juice to melt sugar. Place in pie shell and crisscross dough strips for top. Bake at 350°F until crust is brown and filling is bubbly.

BREAD PUDDING

1 qt. diced bread
3 c. milk
2 c. sugar
¼ lb. butter or margarine

4 eggs
½ c. raisins
¼ tsp. nutmet
¼ tsp. vanilla

Mix all ingredients. Bake at 325°F for approximately 1 hour. Use oven dish.

BAKED APPLES

Peel, core and cut apples into quarters. Put in pot with water and sugar, Let cook until tender. Scoop apples out into a microwaveable pie plate or dish. Sprinkle with more sugar and a little of the water they were cooked in. Drizzle with margarine and sprinkle with apple pie spice. Place in pyrex dish. Bake at 350°F for about 10 minutes.

PERSIMMON PUDDING

2 ½ c. persimmon pulp
1 c. brown sugar
1 c. white (granulated) sugar
3 eggs
½ c. melted butter
3 c. milk

2 c. flour
1 tsp. soda
⅓ tsp. nutmeg
⅓ tsp. cloves
2 tsp. cinnamon

Mix sugar, egg yolks and butter with persimmon pulp. Add sifted dry ingredients alternately with milk. Fold in beaten egg whites. Bake for 1 hour at 350°F.

PERSIMMON PUDDING

2 c. persimmon pulp
1 ½ c. flour
½ c. cornmeal
2 c. sugar
2 c. milk

1 stick margarine
1 tsp. vanilla
2 eggs
pinch of salt

Use baking dish. Mix all ingredients well. Bake 1 hour at 350°F. (Save the corner pieces for me!)

FUDGE DESSERT

4 eggs, beaten
2. c. sugar
¾ c. butter
2 heaping Tbsp. cocoa

½ c. sifted flour pinch of salt
1 c. chopped pecans or walnuts
1 tsp. vanilla

Beat eggs with sugar well. Add cocoa which has dissolved in melted butter. Add flour and other ingredients, except nuts. Beat well. Add nuts Pour in unbuttered pan and place this pan in a pan of water. Bake about 45 minutes at 350°F until crisp on top. Cut into squares or scoop out. Serve with vanilla ice cream.

BANANA PUDDING

3 ½ Tbsp. all-purpose flour
1 ⅓ c. sugar
dash of salt
3 eggs, separated
3 c. milk

1 tsp. vanilla extract
1 (12 oz.) pkg. vanilla wafers
6 med. bananas
¼ c. + 2 Tbsp. sugar
1 tsp. vanilla extract

Combine flour, 1 ⅓ c. sugar and salt in a heavy saucepan. Beat egg yolks; combine egg yolks and milk, mixing well. Stir into dry ingredients; cook over medium heat, stirring constantly, until smooth and thickened. Remove from heat; stir in 1 tsp. vanilla. Layer ⅓ of wafers in a 3-quart baking dish. Since 2 bananas and layer over wafers. Pour ⅓ of custard over bananas. Repeat layers twice. Beat egg whites (at room temperature) until foamy. Gradually add ¼ c. plus 2 Tbsp. sugar, 1 tablespoon at a time, beating until stiff peaks form. Add 1 tsp. vanilla and beat until blended. Spread meringue over custard, sealing to edge of dish. Bake at 425°F for 10 to 12 minutes or until golden brown.

ENGLISH COUNTRY WASSAIL

(Baked Apples in Brandy Sauce)

3 medium oranges
1 Tbsp. whole cloves, optional
1 gal. (16 c.) apple cider
1 qt. (4 c.) cranberry juice cocktail
½ c. sugar
8 sticks cinnamon
1 Tbsp. whole allspice
2 ½ c. rum, optional

Prepare Baked Apples in Brandy Sauce as directed. Meanwhile, stud oranges with cloves, if desired, then cut each orange into ¼-inch-thick slices; set aside.

In an 8-quart Dutch oven, stir together apple cider, cranberry juice and, if desired, aromatic bitters. Add oranges, sugar, stick cinnamon, and allspice.

Bring just to a simmer; reduce heat. Cover and heat for 10 minutes. If desired, stir in dark rum and heat through.

Transfer to large, heat-proof serving bowl. Add baked apples. If desired, stir in the 1 cup reserved brandy sauce from the apples.

Makes about 21 (8 oz.) servings

BAKED APPLES IN BRANDY SAUCE

Core 8 small apples (about 2 lb. total). Peel off a strip around the top of each apple. Place the apples in a 13x9x2- inch baking dish; set aside.

BRANDY SAUCE:

1 c. packed brown sugar
½ tsp. ground cinnamon
¼. tsp. ground nutmeg
⅛ tsp. ground allspice
1 c. brandy

In a small saucepan combine brown sugar, cinnamon, nutmeg and allspice. Stir in brandy. Carefully bring just to boiling over medium-low heat. Pour the brandy sauce over the apples. Cover with foil and bake at 350°F for 25 to 30 minutes or until the apples are just tender when gently tested with a fork.

Use a slotted spoon to remove the apples from the brandy sauce. Reserve 1 cup of the brandy sauce for the wassail. Or, serve apples with sauce as a dessert in individual dessert bowl. Makes 8 servings.

FRESH PEAR COMPOTE

2 Tbsp. wafer crumbs
1 Tbsp. coconut
1 pear, peeled and sliced
¼ c. sugar or honey (or ⅛ & ⅛ each)
3 Tbsp. water

Sprinkle wafer crumbs and coconut into a margarine greased baking dish. Arrange sliced pear over crumbs. Combine sugar/honey and water. Pour into dish over pears. Sprinkle with a few chopped nuts and cinnamon. Bake at 350°F for 20 minutes. (This recipe serves one. To serve more, multiply ingredients by the number of servings. May use up to 8 servings in 1 casserole dish.)

APPLE-DATE NUT BARS

Rotha

2 ½ c. graham cracker crumbs, (fine rolled)
⅓ c. granulated sugar
3 Tbsp. butter, melted
2 Tbsp. water
½ c. ligh.t brown sugar, firmly packed

1 ½. Tbsp. all-purpose flour
½ tsp. baking powder
1 pkg. (8 oz.) chopped dates
1 apple cored and sliced thin
¼ c. chopped walnuts
2 eggs, well beaten

Combine cracker crumbs, granulated sugar, water and butter, blending well. Press firmly into an 8x8x2 inch baking pan.

Combine brown sugar, flour, baking powder, dates, apple, walnuts and eggs. Pour on top of crumb mixture; spread evenly.

Bake at 350°F for 25 minutes or until done. Empty onto a plate 2 minutes after removing from oven cool 10 minutes. Store in an air tight container.

WHITE CHOCOLATE COCONUT BARS

(Light Brownies)

Rotha

First mixture:
6 oz. white chocolate
Melt, combine and set aside.
2 sticks butter

Second mixture:
6 oz. white chocolate, chopped into large pieces
1 sm. pkg. flaked coconut
¼ c. plain flour

Mix well.

Third mixture:
5 eggs, beaten well together
3 c. sugar
1 tsp. coconut flavoring

2 ¼ c. flour, sifted
⅓ c. buttermilk.

Beat eggs and sugar together for 8 minutes; let stand for 3 minutes. Add coconut flavoring. Add *First Mixture*. Slowly mix in flour; add buttermilk. Fold in *Second Mixture*. (Use a large (4 qt.—10x14) or 2 med. (2 qt.—8x10) baking dishes. Grease and line with wax paper. Lightly grease the paper.) Place in 415°F electric oven or 395°F gas oven for approximately 25 to 30 minutes (shorter time with 2 dishes). They will keep cooking after placed on cooking rack. They should be a little less "cakey." This is a brownie type, so don't overcook. Cut while still warm place in an air tight container. These freeze great! A good snack source.

*I use glass Pyrex casserole dishes (1 large or 1 medium). This way I have enough batter still left to make 1 small dish (for a sample!)

BEN'S DATE DELIGHT

Rotha

1 stick butter
⅓ c. sugar
1 c. sifted plain flour
1 pkg. chopped dates
1 c. hot water
2. eggs, well beaten

½ c. oats
½ c. English walnuts
½ c. shredded coconut
⅓ c. plain flour
½ tsp. baking powder

Grease 9x9x.2 pan. Combine butter, sugar and 1 c. plain flour. Put in pan and pack evenly with a fork. Bake for 15 minutes at 350°F. Combine chopped dates with 1 cup hot water; boil for 3 minutes. Pour off most of the water. Mix eggs, oats, walnuts, coconut, ⅓ c. flour and baking powder. Pour evenly over baked crust. Place back into oven and bake at 350°F fur 30 minutes more. Cool and cut into bars. This freezes well.

PETER PAUL MOUND CAKE

1 box Devil Food cake mix
1 can Eagle Brand condensed milk
1 can coconut milk
1 ½ c. flaked coconut
1 (8 oz.) ctn. Cool Whip

Prepare cake mix according to package directions. Bake in 13x9 inch pan. Mix condensed milk and coconut milk together. While cake is hot, punch. holes in cake and pour milk mixture over it. Sprinkle coconut on top. Refrigerate overnight. Top with Cool Whip before serving.

THE BASIC CAKE

Rotha

1 stick butter
1 ½ c. sugar
2 Tbsp. hot water
3 eggs, separated
2 ¼ c. plain flour

2 ¼ tsp. baking powder
1 c. + 2 Tbsp. evaporated milk
½ tsp. vanilla
½ tsp. coconut flavoring

Cream butter with fork. Gradually blend in sugar, by hand. Add hot water. Blend in egg yolks. Sift together 2 times flour and baking powder. Add to creamed mixture alternately with milk and flavorings. Beat after each addition until smooth. Beat egg whites; fold in last. Bake in your choice of pan, floured and greased. Bake at 360°F for 20 to 30 minutes

JELLY ROLL

Use Basic Cake Recipe. Take two 9x13x½-inch cookie sheet. Grease and line with wax paper. Divide cake recipe in ½ for two rolls. Bake at 350°F for 12 minutes.

When cake is baked:

Turn out on confectioner's sugar sprinkled towel. Remove paper. Trim crusts. Roll quickly with fresh sheet of paper on inside of roll. Wrap in sugar-towel and cool.

Unroll, remove paper and ice by spreading with filling or jelly. Roll up. Sprinkle top with coconut or nuts or icing.

FOR LINCOLN LOG: Spread with chocolate frosting and sprinkle with almonds lightly over top side of roll.

BANANA CREAM CAKE

Rotha

Use Basic Cake recipe; fill with mashed banana thinned with whipped cream. Frost with sweetened whipped cream. Dot with well ripened banana slices dipped in lemon juice.

COUNTRY FRUIT CAKE

Rotha

1 lb. butter
12 med.-lg. eggs
4 c. sifted flour
3 tsp. nutmeg
2 tsp. cinnamon
1 c. Karo syrup
1 tsp. soda
1 (10 oz.) pkg. dates, chopped
1 (10 oz.) pkg. figs, chopped
1 (6 oz.) can pineapple, chopped

1 lg. jar marachino cherries, drained
1 box dark raisins
1 box. white raisins
1 box currents
8 lg. pkgs. assorted nuts
1 pkg. dried apples, cooked & mashed
1 pt. (2 c.) figs & ½ of the juice

Dissolve soda in syrup. Mix Basic mixture and add all ingredients. Pour into round pan or Bundt pan. May make 2 cakes. Bake at 350°F for 1 hour 45 minutes until done. Can bake in smaller loaf type pans. Reduce time of cooking to about 1 hour.

FRESH CHOCOLATE-COCONUT CAKE

LAYERS:

3 semi-sweet chocolate squares 1 ½ c. flour
¼ c. water   ¾ tsp. soda
½ c. butter   ½ c. buttermilk
1 ¼ c. sugar   ¼ c. sour cream
3 eggs, separated

Boil together semi-sweet chocolate squares and water until melted. Mix in remaining ingredients adding beaten egg whites last. Bake at 350°F until done.

FROSTING:

¾ c. sugar   1 pkg. frozen coconut,
3 ½ Tbsp. cornstarch   (room temperature)
1 egg yolk, well beaten   ½ c. chopped pecans
1 ¼ c. evaporated milk,   1 tsp. vanilla
(⅓-part water diluted)

Combine sugar and cornstarch, Add egg and milk mixture. Beat with hand mixer until well dissolved and blended. Cook and stir over medium heat about 6 to 8 minutes, until thickened (about like pudding).

Remove from heat, stir in coconut and pecans. Spread over three 8" layers. Use whip cream to ice sides of cake.

OLD TIMEY FUDGE CAKE

Rotha

⅔ c. butter
1 ¾ c. sugar
2 eggs
1 tsp. vanilla

2 ½ (1 oz.) squares unsweetened chocolate, melted
2 ½ c. plain flour, sifted
1 ¼ tsp. soda
1 ¼ c ice water

Cream butter, sugar, eggs and vanilla until fluffy. Beat 5 minutes at high speed, scraping bowl occasionally to guide batter to beaters or beat 5 minutes by hand. Blend in cooled chocolate. Sift together flour and soda. Add flour mixture alternately with ice water. Beat well. Bake in 3 greased cake pans at 350°F for 30 to 35 minutes.

CHOCOLATE ICING

Rotha

4 squares chocolate, light or dark
¾ c. brown sugar, packed
¼ c. butter
⅓ c. water
2 c. confectioner's sugar
2 eggs yolks evaporated milk

Cook together chocolate, brown sugar, butter and water on low heat; simmer until thickened. Cool 10 minutes. Add confectioner's sugar then egg yolks. Blend until thick, whip slightly. Add a small amount of evaporated milk to give desired spreading consistency. Frost cooled cake.

CURIOUS CAKE

1 pkg. (2 layer) German Chocolate cake mix
¾ c. margarine, melted
⅔ c. (5 ⅓ oz. can) evaporated milk
1 c. pecans, chopped
1 pkg. (6 oz.) semisweet chocolate pieces
1 box (14 oz.) caramels

Combine cake mix, margarine and ⅓ c. evaporated milk; mix well. Press half of the mixture onto bottom of 13x9 baking pan. Bake at 350°F for 5 minutes. Sprinkle combined nuts and chocolate pieces over baked crust. Melt caramels with remaining evaporated milk in saucepan over low heat; stir frequently until smooth. Spread caramel mixture evenly over nuts and chocolate pieces. Top with remaining cake mixture; press gently. Bake at 350°F for 20 minutes; cool slightly. Refrigerate.

WHITE CHOCOLATE CHEESECAKE

1 (8 oz.) pkg. softened cream cheese
2 sm. pkgs. white chocolate instant jello pudding mix
2 c. cold milk
8 oz. Cool Whip
1 graham cracker pie crust

Beat cream cheese and ½ c. milk; add remaining 1 ½ c. milk and pudding mix. Beat with wire whisk for one minute. Stir in Cool Whip until smooth and well blended. Spoon into crust. Refrigerate 4 hours or overnight.

PINEAPPLE UPSIDE-DOWN CAKE

Rotha

In sauce pan, melt:
4 Tbsp. butter   ¾ c. brown sugar

Pour into greased and floured baking pan (10x10x2). Arrange slices of pineapple in bottom of pan and sprinkle in ¼ c. nuts. Use Basic Cake recipe. (This size will use ½ the recipe or make two square layers and fill between with pineapple jelly.) Bake at 350°F for 20 minutes or until done. Serve upside-down with whipped cream.

SPECIAL COCONUT POUND CAKE

Rotha

2 sticks butter or margarine
½ c. Crisco
3 c. sugar
6 eggs
3 ½ tsp. almond flavoring
3 tsp. coconut flavoring
3 c. all-purpose flour
1 c. milk (½ sweet milk & ½ evaporated)
1 (8 oz.) pkg. flaked coconut

Cream butter, shortening and sugar until light and fluffy. Add eggs, one at a time; beat well after each. Add flavorings; blend well. Alternately add flour and milk, beating well. Stir in coconut. Spoon batter into greased and floured Bundt pan or tube pan. Bake at 350°F for 1 hour and 15 minutes.

YUM-YUM CAKE

1 c. plain, whole wheat flour
1 c. sugar or
¾ tsp. baking soda
1 egg, slightly beaten
½ tsp. vanilla
1 can (8 ¾ oz.) fruit cocktail, not drained
½ c. chopped nuts

Mix all ingredients together in 8x8x2 inch ungreased cake pan. Bake at 350°F for 30 minutes. Frost immediately.

FROSTING:

¼ c. soft butter or margarine
1 pkg. (3 oz.) cream cheese, softened
1 c. confectioners' sugar, sifted
½ tsp. vanilla

Blend all ingredients until smooth.

GENUINE OLD FASHIONED POUND CAKE

1 lb. (2 c.) sugar
1 lb. (10) eggs, separated
1 tsp. vanilla
1 lb. butter

2 tsp. orange or lemon extract
1 lb. all-purpose flour, (sifted 3 ¾ c.)

Cream butter and beat in sugar gradually; cream well. Add egg yolks slowly; beat thoroughly. Add vanilla and extract lightly and fold in sifted flour. Beat egg whites until barely stiff and fold in gently. Pour into 10" tube pan lined with wax paper. Bake for 1 ½ hours at 330°F.

RUM CAKE

2 c. chopped walnuts
1 (18 ½ oz.) pkg. yellow cake mix with pudding
3 eggs
½ c. cold water
⅓ c. vegetables oil
½ c. dark rum or spiced rum

Preheat 1 cup nuts over bottom of pan. Mix all ingredients together. Add 1 cup floured walnuts. Pour batter over nuts.

Bake 1 hour; cool. Invert on serving dish. Prick top.

Spoon and brush glaze evenly over top and sides slowly, allowing cake to absorb glaze. Repeat until all glaze is used up.

GLAZE:

¼ lb. butter
¼ c. water
1 c. granulated sugar
¼ c. rum

Melt butter in saucepan. Stir in water and sugar. Boil 5 minutes stirring constantly. Remove from heat; add rum.

ON THE ROAD SPECIAL CAKE

1 box yellow cake mix
2 eggs
1 stick oleo
1 lb. box xxx sugar

1 (8 oz.) pkg. cream cheese
2 eggs
½ c. chopped pecans

Mix cake mix, 2 eggs and oleo. Place in 10x14-inch greased pan. Mix 1 box of xxx sugar (minus 3 Tbsp.), cream cheese and 2 eggs. Pour over first layer. Sprinkle with chopped pecans. and 3 Tbsp. reserved sugar. Place in cold oven. Bake at 325°F for 45 minutes to 1 hour. Cut into squares.

APPLESAUCE CAKE

4 eggs
2 c. sugar
1 c. butter
3 c. applesauce
4 c. plain flour
1 c. chopped walnuts

1 c. finely chopped apples
3 tsp. soda
3 Tbsp. cocoa
½ tsp. cinnamon
1 tsp. vanilla

Mix sugar and butter well. Add eggs and mix. Add soda, cocoa. and cinnamon to flour and sift. Add applesauce and flour mixture and beat well. Add walnuts, raisins and vanilla. Bake in tube pan at 325°F for 1 hour. Test with toothpick.

FRESH APPLE CAKE

3 c. finely chopped apples	2 eggs
3 Tbsp. lemon juice	3 c. flour
3 tsp. cinnamon	1 tsp. salt
2 c. sugar	1 tsp. soda
1 ¼ c. vegetable oil or butter	2 tsp. vanilla

Beat sugar, oil and eggs until creamy. Sift flour, salt and soda together. Add to creamed mixture a little at a time, until all is mixed. Will be very stiff. Add apples and vanilla. Spread in a greased and floured 13x9 inch pan. Bake at 350°F for 35 minutes. Do not overcook.

GLAZE: Combine 3 tablespoons lemon juice with 1 cup confectioner's sugar. Pour over cake when done.

GERMAN CHOCOLATE CAKE

1 stick butter
1 ¼ c. brown sugar
2. eggs, separated, plus 2 whites
1 tsp. vanilla
½ pkg. German chocolate
¼ c. water
1 tsp. soda
1 ¼ c. cake flour
½ c. buttermilk

Soften butter; blend in sugar and egg yolks. Whip with heavy fork until smooth and fluffy.
Add and stir in chocolate. Alternate flour and soda (sifted together) and buttermilk. Beat egg whites until foamy; stir in. Grease and flour two 9-inch cake, pans and pour batter into these. Bake at 340°F about 35 minutes. When done, let cool 5 minutes then turn onto towel and frost in 10 minutes. Keep finished cake in an airtight container for freshness and moistness.

PECAN/COCONUT FROSTING

1 c. evaporated milk
1 c. sugar
3 egg yolks
½ stick butter
1 Tbsp. coconut flavoring
1 sm. pkg. coconut
1 c. chopped pecans

BASIC FROSTING

Rotha

2 c. confectioner's sugar
½ stick butter, melted

3 to 4 Tbsp. undiluted evaporated milk
2 tsp. flavoring

Blend until smooth at a good spreading consistency.

*Add flavoring of your choice. If you desire color, add the color of your choice.

CHOCOLATE-NUT FROSTING

Rotha

Use Basic Frosting recipe.

Add:

½ tsp. red cake coloring   ¾ Q. walnuts, chopped
2 cubes chocolate,
(melt with butter)

Blend all ingredients together and spread evenly over layers and sides of cake. Frost while cake is warm.

Combine evaporated milk, sugar, egg yolks, butter and flavoring. Cook and stir occasionally over medium heat, 10 to 15 minutes until thick.
Add coconut and pecans. Stir well and spread after cooling slightly.

DATE NUT ICING

½ pkg. chopped dates
½ c. flaked coconut
½ c. brown sugar

½ c. + 2 Tbsp. can milk
2 Tbsp. margarine

Combine all ingredients in sauce pan. Heat and beat with fork as it cooks, about 6 to 8 minutes, until blended smoothly.

APPLE LAYER CAKE

Rotha

LAYERS:

1 ½ C. oil
3 eggs
2 c. sugar
1 tsp. vanilla
3 c. plain flour

1 tsp. soda
1 tsp. salt
3 c. diced apples
1 c. nuts
1 ½ c. coconut

Beat first 4 ingredients with mixer. Sift in flour, soda and salt. Fold in apples, nuts, and coconut.

Bake at 350°F for 30 minutes (3 layers).

FILLING:

1 ⅓ c. brown sugar
⅓ c. milk

4 Tbsp. Karo syrup
3 to 4 Tbsp. butter

Combine filling ingredients and bring to a boil; remove from heat and let cool completely.

BUMPY CHOCOLATE FUDGE POUND CAKE

Rotha

2 sticks butter
1 stick margarine
6 eggs
½ tsp. soda
½ c. buttermilk

1 pkg. Rich 'n Moist Brownie Mix
2 c. plain flour
1 ½ c. pecan pieces
1 pkg. frozen coconut
1 ½ c. sugar

Cream butter and margarine until smooth. Add eggs, one at a time. Combine soda and buttermilk Stir into creamed mixture. Add brownie mix, reserve ¾ cup. Add 1 ½ cups plain flour, reserving ½ cup.

Dust pecan pieces with reserved ½ cup flour. Add rolled pecans and coconut to batter.

Bake in greased and floured Bundt pan at 360°F for 1 hour and 10 minutes Cool 20 minutes and frost while still warm.

FROSTING:

314. c. Rich. 'n Moist Brownie mix (reserved from batter recipe)
½ c. butter
2 blocks semi-sweet chocolate
¼ c. milk

Melt semi-sweet chocolate in microwave for 2 minutes. Combine with brownie mix, butter and milk. Frost cake. (May streak with powdered sugar mixed with a little milk.)

BLACK WALNUT-RUM POUND CAKE

3 sticks butter, softened
1 (16 oz.) pkg. light brown sugar
1 c. sugar
5 eggs
¾ c. milk.
¼ c. light rum (Barcardi)

2 Tbsp. pure vanilla extract
2 Tbsp. pure vanilla extract
3 c. all-purpose flour, sifted
1 tsp. baking powder
1 c. black walnuts, chopped

Cream butter and sugars together. Beat each egg, one at a time. Combine milk, rum and vanilla; set aside. Combine and sift flour and baking powder; set aside.

Alternate. liquid and dry mixture ending with about the last cup of flour. Blend well after each addition. Stir in nuts. Put into greased and floured tube or Bundt cake pan. Place in center of 350°F oven for 1 hour and 15 minutes. Check doneness.

When done, place on rack 10 to 15 minutes then turn onto cake plate. Let cool 30 minutes then cover in air tight container for 2 hours. Frost while still warm.

FROSTING:

2 c. confectioners' sugar 2 Tbsp. orange juice
1 Tbsp. Amonetto liquor

Combine all ingredients and stir to spreading consistency. (Add more orange juice if needed.) Frost cake.

SIMPLE COOKIES

1 box brown sugar
3 eggs
3 c. unsifted flour
¼ tsp. salt

1 tsp. baking powder
¼ tsp. soda
1 c. shortening
1 tsp. lemon flavoring

Combine all ingredients. Drop (or make into a roll and slice) on greased cookie sheet. Bake at 375°F for 10 to 15 minutes.

FRUIT CAKE COOKIES

1 c. brown sugar
3 c. plain flour
3 eggs
½ tsp. cinnamon
½ tsp. cloves
½ tsp. nutmeg
1 lb. candied pineapple

1 lb. candied cherries,
red & green
1 lb. dates, chopped
1 c. butter
½ C. milk
1 Tbsp. soda
7 c. chopped pecans & walnuts

Cut cherries in fourths. Chip pineapple. Cream sugar and butter; add eggs. Sift dry ingredients and mix with creamed mixture, a small amount at a time. Add milk; mix well Add fruits and nuts. Drop by tablespoonsful onto greased cookie sheets. Bake at 325°F. for 15 minutes.

LACE COOKIES

⅓ c. butter
⅔ c. packed brown sugar
1 Tbsp. flour
¼ tsp. salt

1 Tbsp. milk
lemon or orange peel
1 c. raw oatmeal (add more milk if needed)

Beat butter and sugar. Add flour, salt, milk and peel. Beat well; add oats and stir. Drop by level teaspoonful's onto ungreased cookie sheet, 2 inches apart. Bake at 350°F for about 7 minutes.

FUDGE

⅔ c. milk
2 sq. baking chocolate unsweetened
2 c. sugar
1 tsp. com syrup

dash of salt
2 Tbsp. butter
1 tsp. vanilla
1 c. chopped nuts

Melt chocolate in milk over low heat and mix until smooth. Stir in sugar and salt; cook gently to 236°F.

Remove from heat; add butter and cool without stirring to lukewarm. Add vanilla and nuts. Beat until thick and no longer glassy. Pour in pan; cut into squares.

SIMPLE COOKIES

2 c. sugar
½ stick margarine
½ c. cocoa
½ c. water

½ c. coconut
½ c. peanut butter
1 tsp. vanilla
2 c. uncooked quick oats

Combine sugar, margarine, cocoa, water and coconut. Stir constantly over low heat for two minutes when it starts boiling, Remove from heat and stir in peanut butter and vanilla. Mix well and pour over oats. Drop onto waxed paper and cool.

MONSTER COOKIES

1 c. butter
1 lb. brown sugar (2 ¼ c. packed)
2 c. granulated sugar
6 eggs
2 c. peanut butter
4 tsp. soda

1 tsp. vanilla
1 tsp. light corn syrup
½ lb. raisins
1 c. chopped nuts
½ lb. chocolate chips
9 c. quick cooking oatmeal

Blend together butter, sugars and eggs. Add peanut butter, soda, vanilla, corn syrup; blend well. Add raisins, nuts, chocolate chips and oatmeal. Drop by teaspoonfuls onto greased cookie sheets (larger spoonfuls make chewier cookies) and bake at 325°F to 350°F for 8 to 12 minutes.

SWEET CHOCOLATE DOUBLE-DECK BROWNIES

⅔ c. unsifted all-purpose flour
½ tsp. double-acting baking powder
¼ tsp. salt
⅔ c. sugar
2 eggs, well beaten

⅓ c. butter or shortening melted
⅓ c. flaked coconut
½ tsp. almond extract
1 pkg. (4 oz.) sweet cooking chocolate, melted

Mix flour with baking powder and salt. Gradually add sugar to eggs, beating thoroughly. Blend in butter. Add flour mixture and mix well. Pour ½ cup of batter into a small bowl; stir in coconut and almond extract. Add chocolate to remaining batter and spread evenly in greased 8-inch square pan. Drop coconut batter by teaspoonfuls over chocolate batter in pan; then spread carefully to form a thin even layer. Bake at 350°F for 30 to 35 minutes or until lightly browned. Cool in pan on rack. Cut in bars or squares Makes about 20.

HONEY-NUT BALLS

2 c. powdered milk 1 c. honey
1 c. crunchy peanut butter ½ tsp. coconut flavoring

Mix all ingredients. Roll in chopped pecans and into small balls. Chill. For use at parties, place a toothpick in each and serve on trays. (Add 2 squares of chocolate for another version.)

BATCHELOR BUTTON COOKIES

1 c. butter
1 c. light brown sugar
1 egg, well beaten
½ tsp. salt

2 c. plain flour
1 tsp. soda
1 c. coconut
1 c. chopped pecans

Cream butter and sugar. Add egg, beat well. Sift together salt, soda and flour. Add to creamed mixture. Add coconut and pecans. Chill approximately 2 hours. Roll into balls. Bake at 375°F for about 10 minutes. Don't overbake.

KILLER BROWNIES

Rotha

1 (8 oz.) pkg. chocolate blocks
2 sticks butter
5 eggs
3 ½ c. sugar
2 Tbsp. vanilla
¼ tsp. salt

¼ tsp. baking powder
2 ⅓ c. sifted flour
⅓ c. buttermilk
1 ¼ c. chopped nuts or chocolate, floured
1 ½ c. slivered almonds

Melt chocolate and butter slowly. Add eggs, 1 at a time, to sugar, vanilla, salt and baking powder; beating 10 minutes total. Add alternately to chocolate mixture the flour and buttermilk. Add floured nuts or chocolate. Pour into greased, wax paper lined, greased and floured (2 medium) baking dishes. Sprinkle top with slivered almonds. Bake at 425°F for 25 to 30 minutes.

NEW COOKIE

Rotha

1 c. peaches
½ c. pecans
½ c. almonds
¼ c. coconut or
¼ c. wheat germ
8 figs, chopped

¼ c. molasses sugar (¼ c. brown sugar)
1 egg
1 c. flour, sifted
½ stick margarine

Blend peaches, pecans, almonds, and coconut. Add figs and sugar; blend well. Add egg, flour and margarine. Drop by teaspoonfuls onto greased cookie sheets. Bake at 350°F for 25 to 35 minutes.

NEW YORK TEA TIME COOKIES

Babylon, NY

½ c. plain flour
½ tsp. salt
1 ½ c. butter

1 c. sugar
2 egg yolks
2 tsp. vanilla

Sift together flour and salt; set aside. Blend together butter and sugar. Add egg yolks and vanilla. Add flour mixture. Put thru cookie. press onto ungreased cookie sheet. Bake at 375°F for 10 minutes.

ROTHA'S PRECIOUS COOKIES

Rotha

1 stick butter
12 Tbsp. sugar, (white and brown)
1 egg
1 tsp. almond extract

1 c. + 4 Tbsp. sifted flour
½ tsp. soda
1 c. chopped nuts
1 c. flaked coconut
½ c. oatmeal

Combine until creamy, butter, sugars, egg and almond extract. Add flour and soda. Stir in chopped nuts coconut and oatmeal. Decorate top with chocolate bits or cherries. Bake at 350°F for 30 minutes.

SUGAR COATED PEANUTS

2 c. sugar
½ c. water

2 c. raw, shelled peanuts with skins

Dissolve sugar in water in saucepan over medium heat. Add peanuts and continue to cook over medium heat for about 10 minutes, stirring frequently. Cook and stir until peanuts are completely coated and no syrup is left. Spread on ungreased cookie sheet. Bake at 300°F for 30 minutes, stirring at 3 minute intervals.

RED'S THEORY OF GOOD LIVING

We live in a very complicated world today. Seems as if there really is no time to cook or time to sit down to enjoy a meal. Fast food, drive-through and at-home-box-prepared has jumped into our lives. Certainly, occasionally and in haste, this is needed but it should never take over.

We must take time to make a few plans to get back to a similarity of those good old days. As families, we, move in such varied directions, yet, there is nothing to compare to sitting down at your own table and testing a new recipe, a new dessert, or just plain good home cooking.

A meal is more than just food… It is also a time to gather your thoughts and spend a special time with those around you. If you are alone, it is excellent to plan some meals around some television that entertains you. I take this time for news or even a tape that I need to view or hear.

A great portion of our population is on the road. With a truckdriver, salesman and various travel oriented professions, eating habits are put in a bind. But, this can change.

Many professional people are caught in the same old trap. It is a quick answer to grab on the go, but it can be habit forming. Us Southern folks know this 'epidemic' was cast upon us by the

Yankee; but, then where did the Kentucky Fried Chicken come from? Well, we won't dwell on those 'who' s' and it is not all bad. But it is unreal to be driving down the road trying to steer your vehicle and eat, too.

RED'S THEORY 2

So, how do we do this? This book is pulled together to give you some of the best and not such difficult recipes for you to try. Select a couple cakes for instance, make them. Eat some for the next couple of meals and freeze the rest. I like to take my pound cakes and slice them into about 22 pieces. I wrap each piece individually in clear plastic wrap and usually freeze a dozen pieces for later. (Place these 'saved cake slices' in an additional freezer bag together.) Most of the time, I keep a chocolate pound cake, a coconut pound cake, a batch of brownies and gooey bars sliced and frozen. Its there for unexpected guests or better still, when I hit the road for parts unknown, I have it ready. The frozen cakes are even better than ever. A zap in the microwave and it is wonderful!

I prepare many foods in the same way. Using many of the recipes in the cook book, I prepare and sort into portions and freeze. I use containers that are disposable if I am on the road and don't want to deal with dirty dishes. As well, most disposable containers will go into a microwave. A microwave in your vehicle is great, but fuel stops have them too and are glad for you to use them.

Not so long ago, I had some of my yeast rolls, lasagne, beets and peaches that I had canned, and several pieces of coconut cake. In a road stop, I started heating things. The aroma drifted out through the people trying to pick a cold sandwich to warm. One man almost ran to me saying, "Where did you get that?"

He thought it was from the place. I had a bit extra with me and ultimately, I ended up feeding four truckers who had not had a home cooked meal in months. That was a satisfying as anything, I explained to them, how I did it. They swore they were going to change their eating habits. One of them called me later and asked for a recipe and thanked me.

RED'S THEORY 3

Still, I love to get even crazier. I like to get into this cook book and make preserves. It is easy and so good. Canning, freezing and preserving is important. It is cheaper, but more than cost, it tastes great. And there is the fact of doing it yourself.

We go into a grocery store and it takes very little to spend a hundred dollars. Take the time to plan. It will help.

In the theory, I believe there is a great chance that we are headed for some tough times. Our national budget is so out of whack and we are truly in the dark about the truth of our country's real economical status. Something tells me to be like a squirrel and plan for that possibility. It is very possible that we might come to a time that we have to really budget and be careful.

We need to start learning to buy food and prepare it without waste. Get away from the boxes and get simple. Try a pot of beans and buy at the farmer's market. It's fun anyhow and when those around you get such pleasure from your cooking skills, it is even greater.

And if you wish to really get into my web of rationalization, I also believe we may need to learn to grow whatever we can. This year I did just a little planting and had tomatoes, peppers, cucumbers, potatoes, onions, green beans, peas and greens. I had all I needed and still shared and traded. Never underestimate anything.

I enjoyed my plants. Much more fun than flowers! I like to eat my efforts, not sniff and look at them!

It is something to think about. What would you do if our world. as we know it, came tumbling down? Are you a survivor? Our hopes don't want to ever address this, yet it is scary to think. You can bet, when the rich man is hit with loss, heads will roll. My theory, and I want you to share these thoughts, is learn to live simple. Be able to cut the unnecessary and prepare. Have an economical house and get it paid for. Learn to live off the land and do your own thing. Get your job security from getting settled in a position where you are needed. We had better start finding some place to start digging gold to back the money we spend.

RED'S THEORY 4

Even if I am wrong, anything I save would be mine. I try to think before I just throw away. Before I buy, do I 'need' it? We all have boxes of nostalgia, things we keep hanging on to.

I hope you will enjoy this cook book and maybe it will keep the old and basic close to you. In our grandparents and parent's day, and even mine, most of this type cooking was fit for the preacher! And you know, we are all special and we deserve to enjoy the best of food! This is a collection of the things I love! There are many other recipes in my desk, but these are my favorites.

As you go along, you will collect certain recipes that extend your cooking ability. Many of us collect cook books. They are neat to just read. But in the kitchen, that's where the facts lay waiting.

Many of these recipes can be cooked anywhere. Often, I cook on a two burner camp stove. You just improvise to make it happen. Guess it is a matter of loving to eat good food! I live alone, but I don't neglect cooking.

The theory… Eat, cook, enjoy and be healthy no matter what!

Keep cookin'!

www.ingramcontent.com/pod-product-compliance
Lightning Source LLC
LaVergne TN
LVHW010200070526
838199LV00062B/4426